Messages D'Amour

Reflections Of Love

MESSAGES D'AMOUR - Reflections of Love

Premier Edition Published in 2015 in the United States of America

WWW.MYDOVESONG.COM

ISBN-13: 978-0692022023
ISBN-10: 0692022023

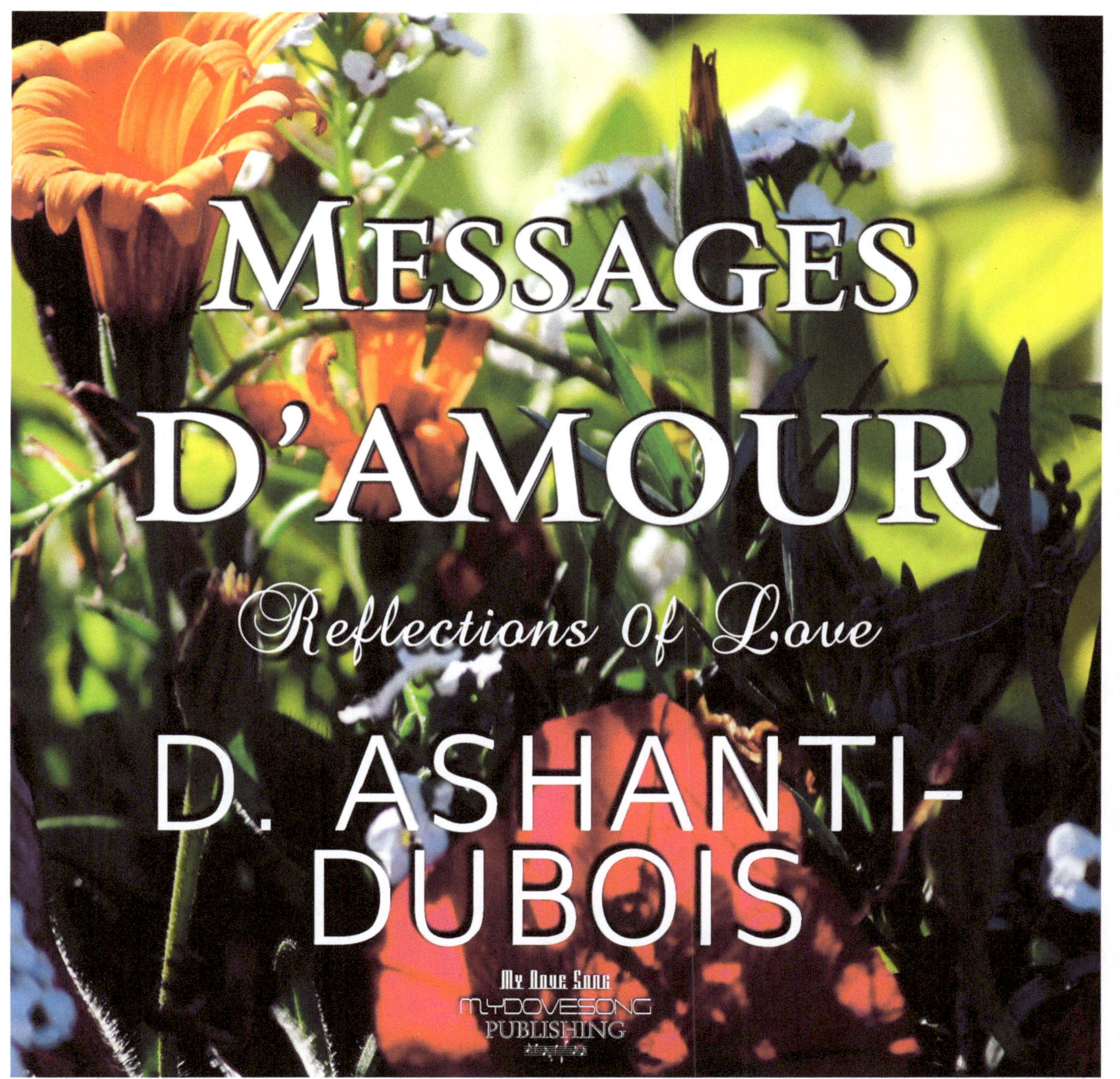
MESSAGES
D'AMOUR
Reflections Of Love
D. ASHANTI-
DUBOIS
My Dove Song
MYDOVESONG
PUBLISHING

When I breathe, your love woos me and I dance within myself like the wind waltzing with the willow; swaying tenderly like the leaves on the trees. And I feel happy to be alive because you free me. I am the luckiest person alive because you chose me... Thank you... Thank you, my beloved, for loving me...

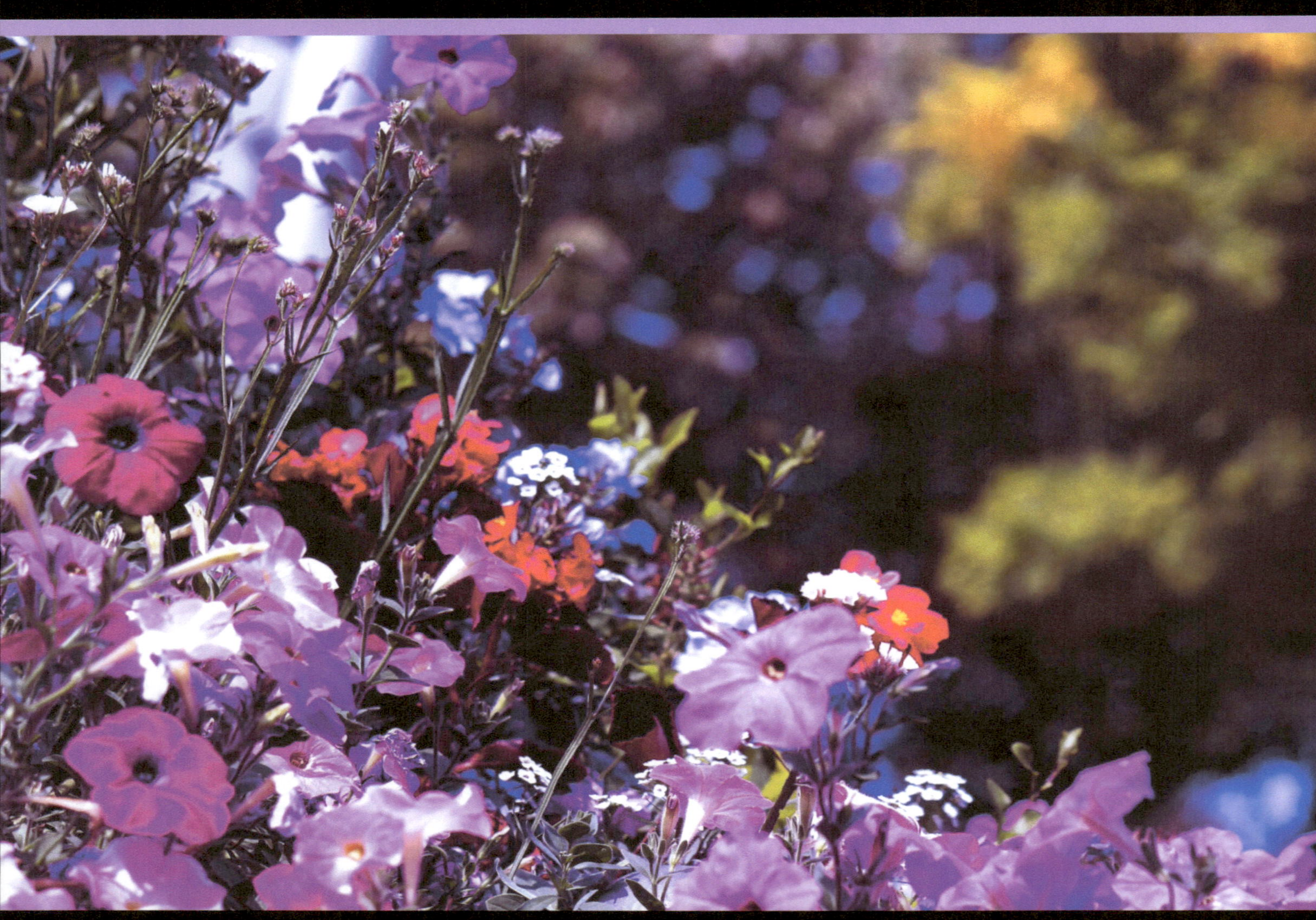

Your luminous gaze... Your loving smile... You never ceases to amaze me. I can see your face with my eyes closed shut. I only need to think of you, and you appear. For your heart touches my heart and we succinctly breathe as one. Whether you're near or far away, my love will burn unquenchably for you... For you are my everlasting love...

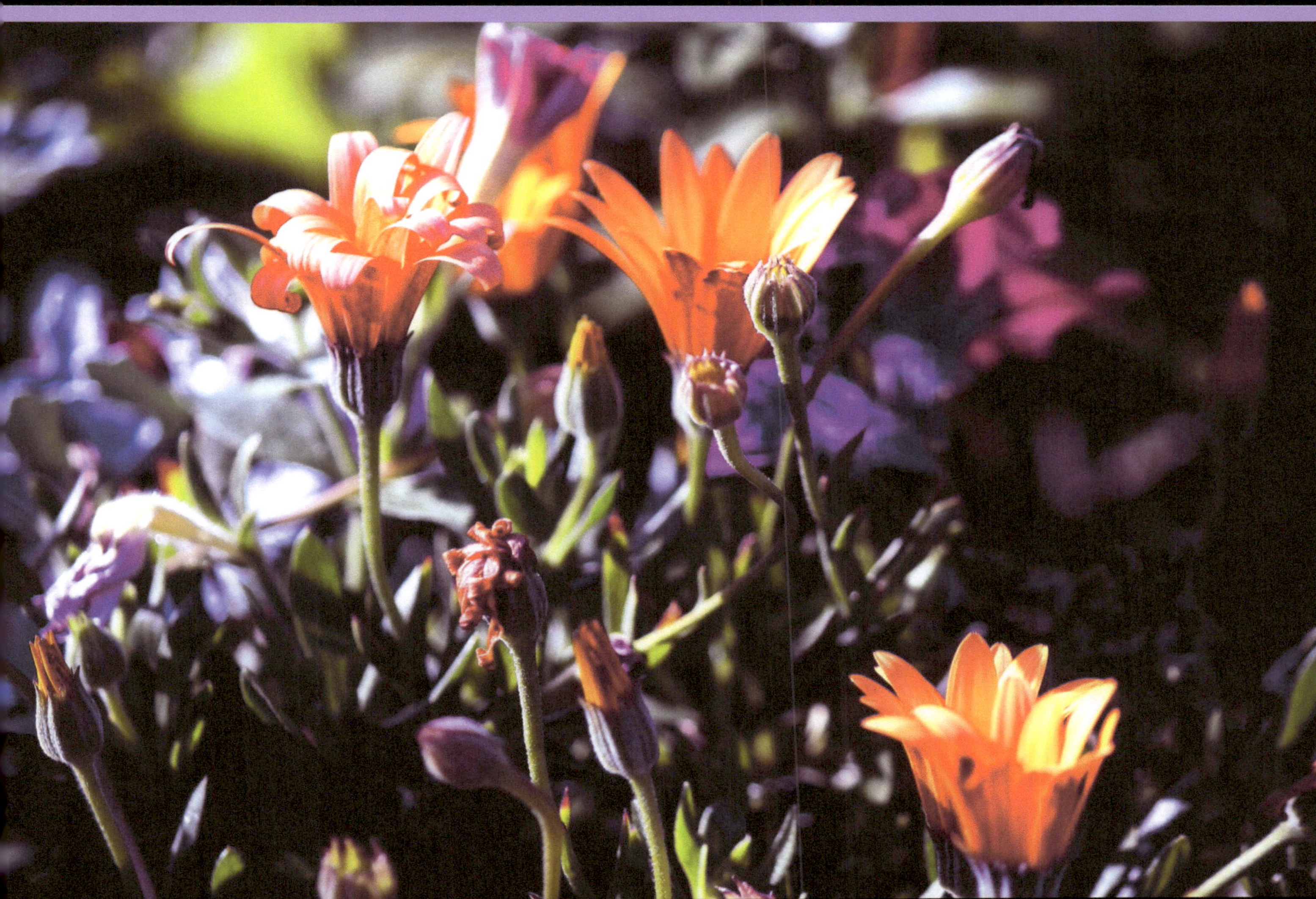

Lean close upon my breasts... Tell me what your heart beckons for. Is it love that you desire? My dreams are for your dreams to come true, and my wishes are for your wishes to manifest. Whisper your soul to me like a hummingbird to a succulent rose. Let me be your confident; your love is safe with me...

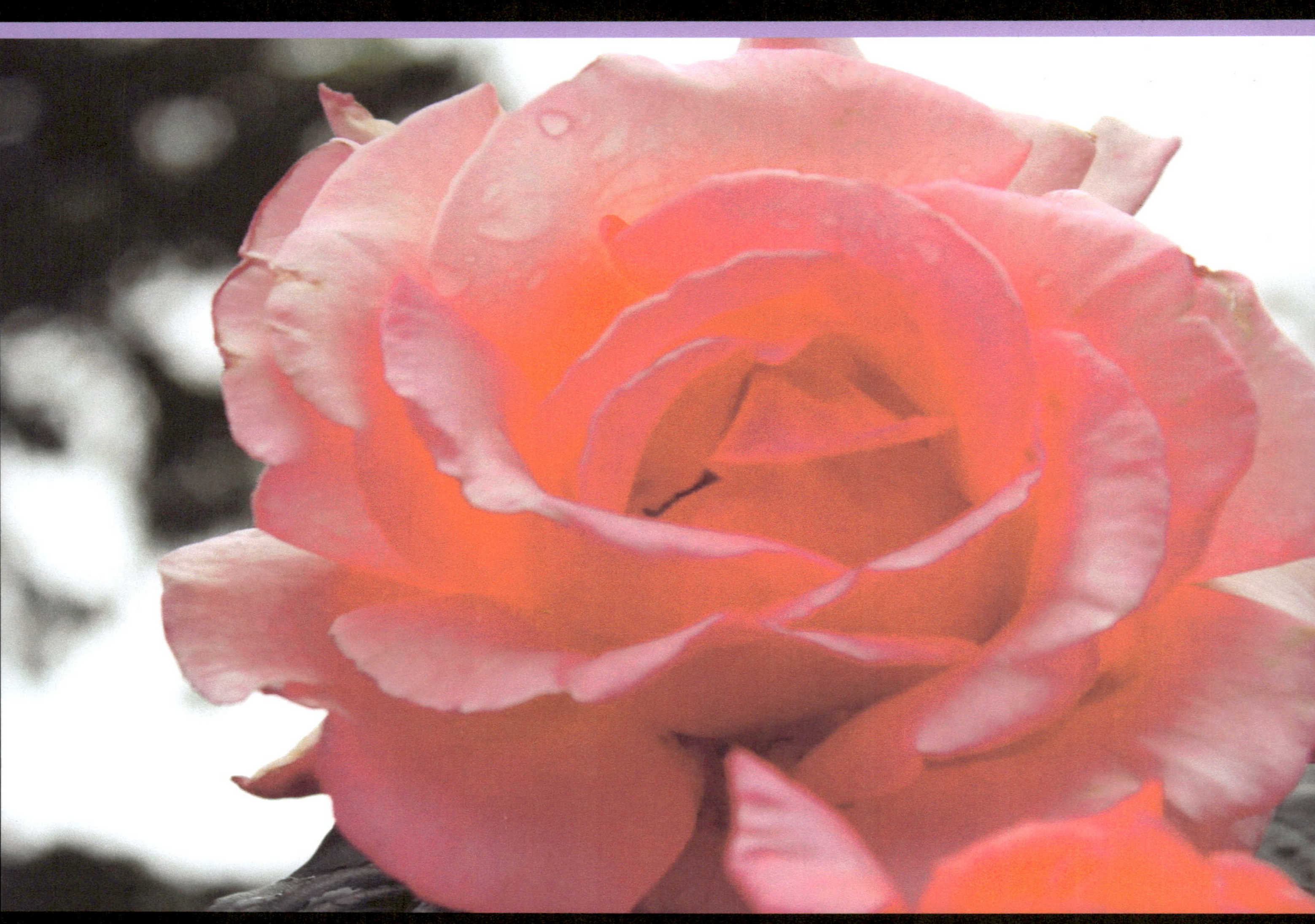

How I love you... How I really do... Finally, you belong to me and I belong to you... How I missed you when you were away, but now you're loving me, so tenderly and our love is here to stay. And as sure as I am breathing, our loves never-ending. I promise you now face to face... I promise you forever... Love is here to stay...

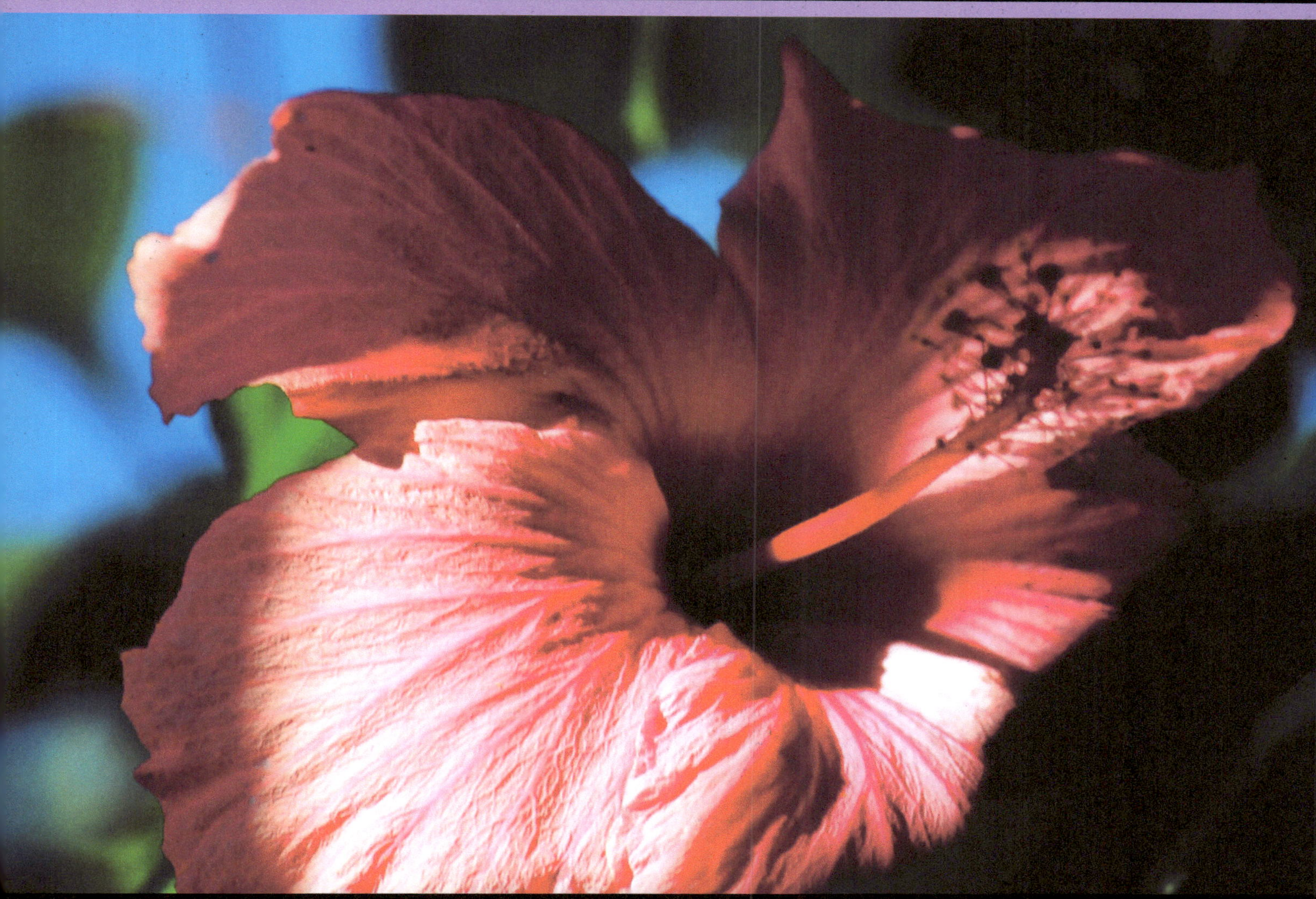

Here in the sight of God, I give my love to you, and I promise that you and I are one. You'll never be lonely because you are inside me; holding me, loving me, sharing eternity. We will be lovers for all time. And for time, my heart will belong to you, and your dreams will be my dreams, too. Together we'll take the high road and leave behind the lonely memories and love will bind us in a sacred grace...

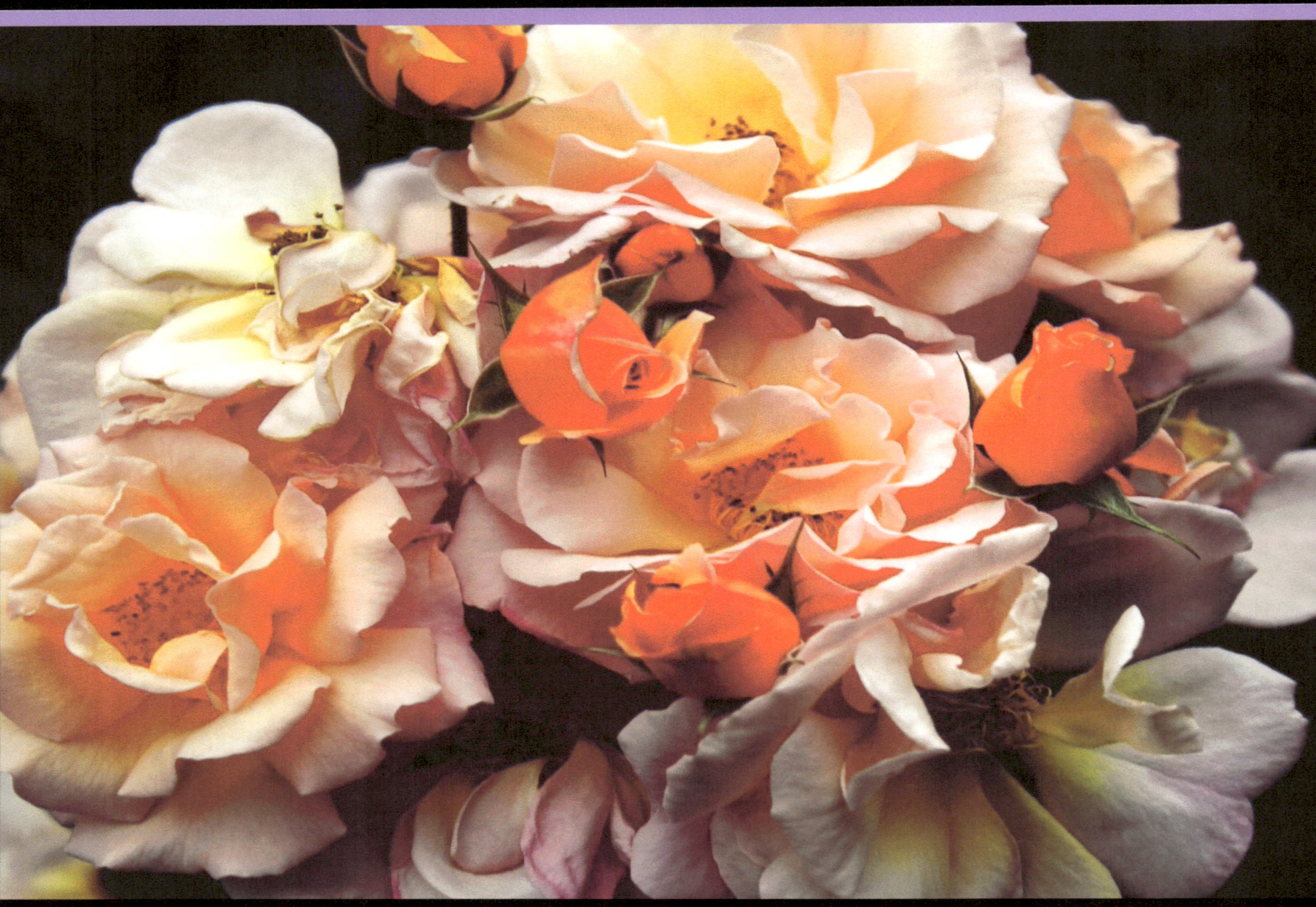

How sweet you are, as you throw your arms about me and softy kiss my face. There is none other whom I would rather give my love to. You complete me with just a warm embrace. You encompass my very soul. How much love can one give? How much more can one adore? You prove time and again that love is limitless, and I will love you until time is no more...

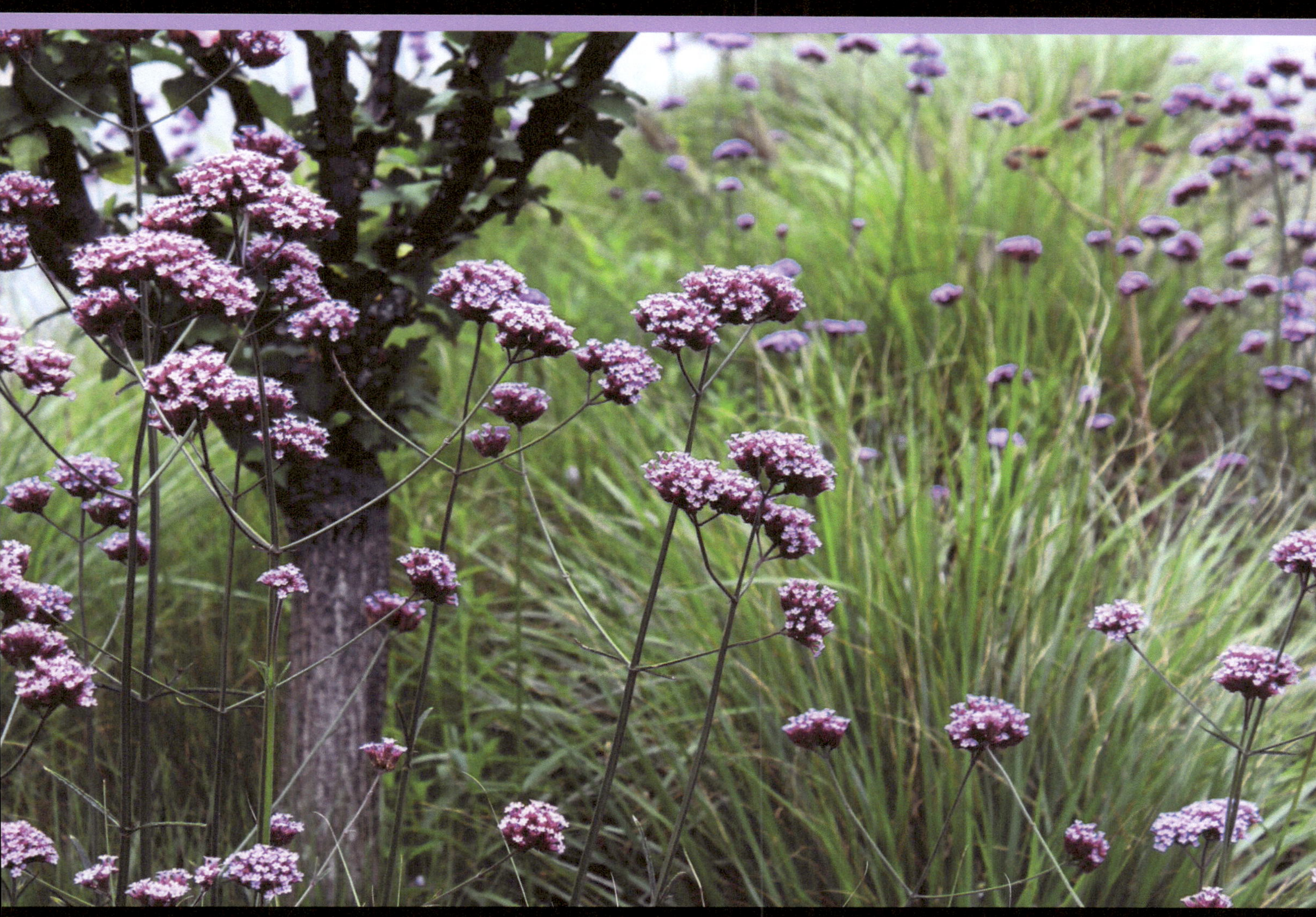

Close your eyes... Do you see what I see? There are butterflies wafting all about you. And that perfume... The sweet whiff of vanilla rose... What a wonderful succulent perfume...the fragrance of your soul; the aroma of l'amour. Can you taste it? It's on the tip of my tongue. Your kiss... The intoxicating taste of love...

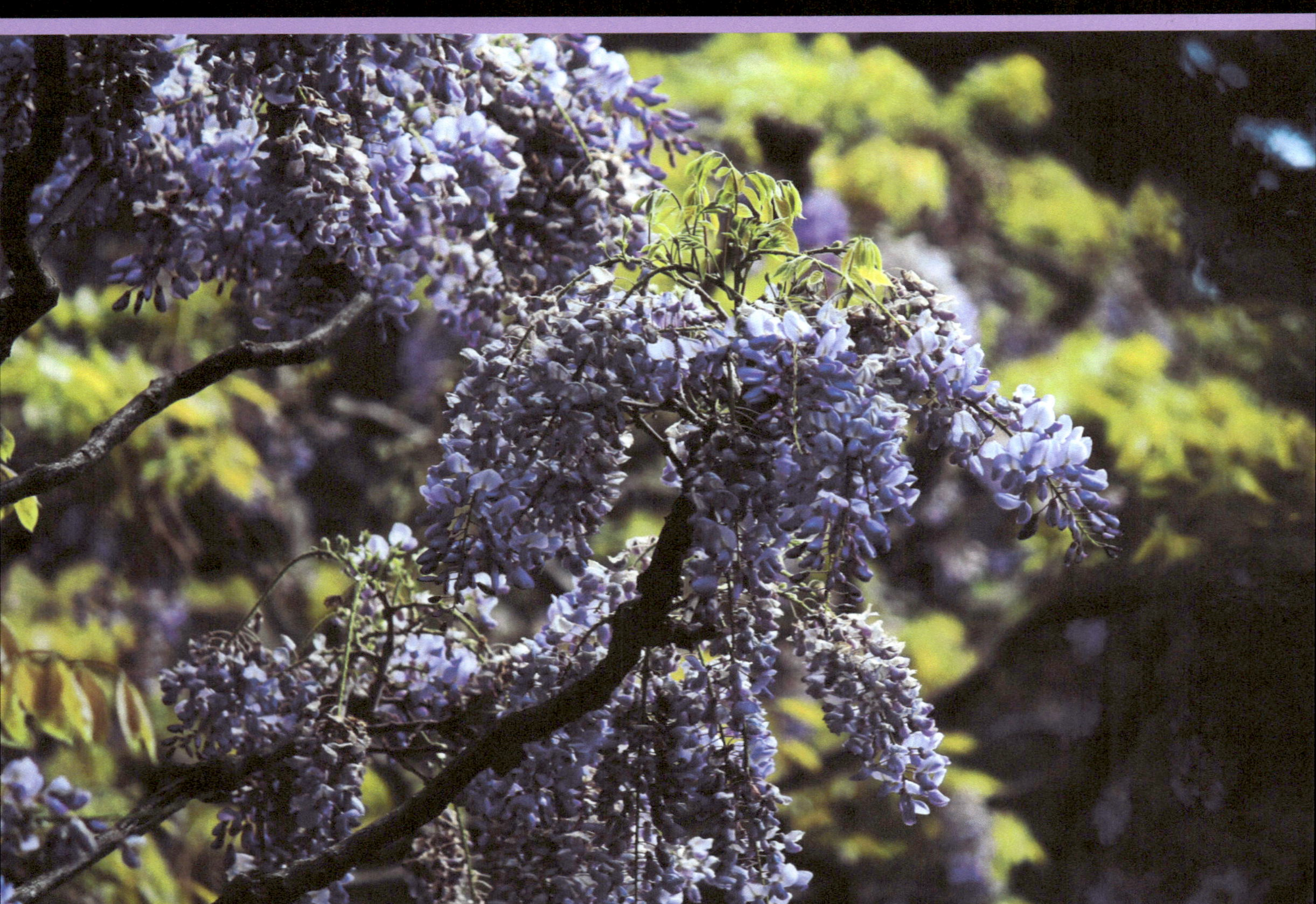

Without love, we are empty vessels waiting to be filled. How lucky I am... You keep me sane in this mad world. Where would I be without out your beautiful peace? Yours, mine, ours as one. Together we make life the joy it was meant to be. You, my passion, my partner through time; you are my fortune, my true love, my prize... And I can't imagine my life without you...

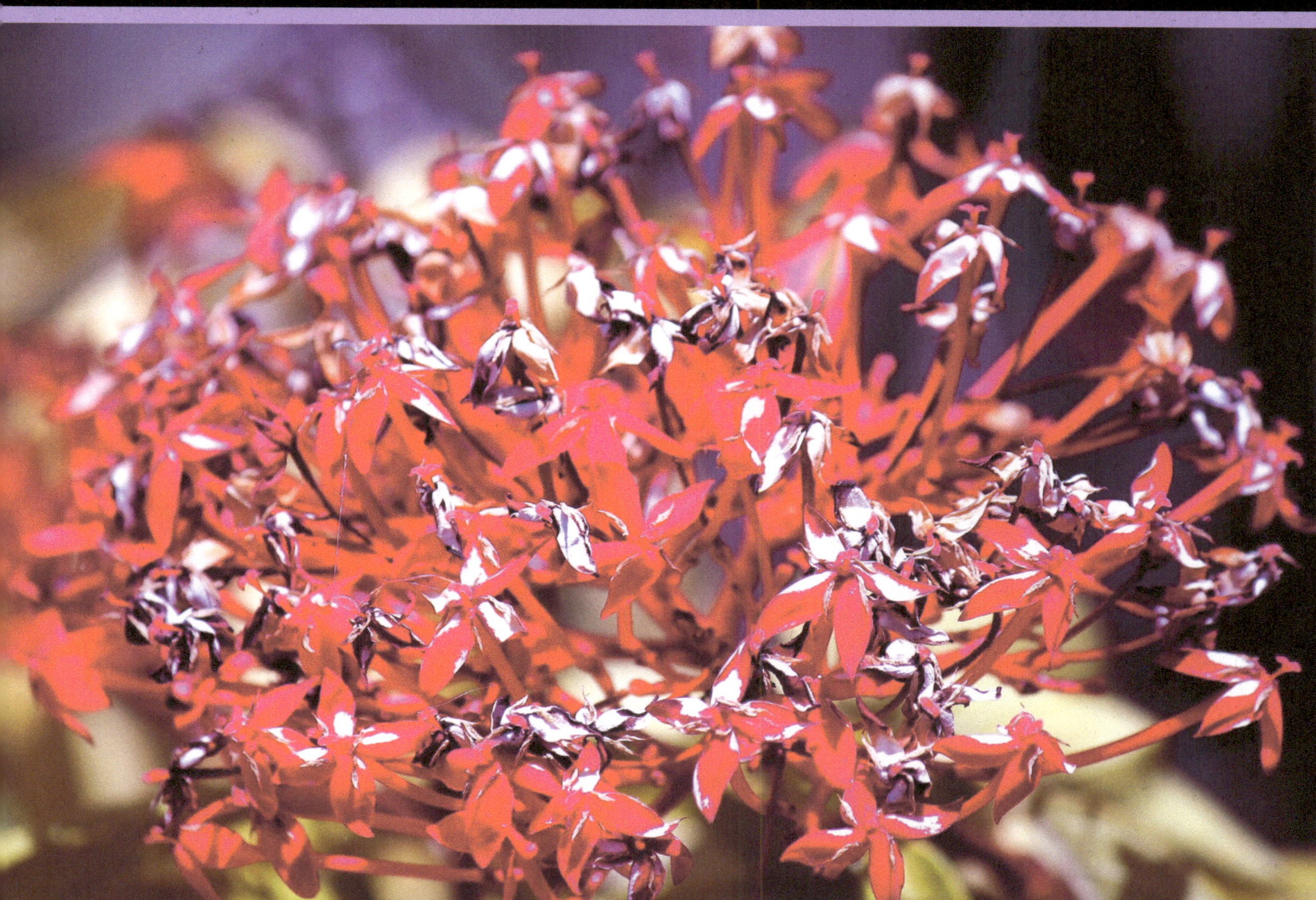

You are a multifaceted diamond, an iridescent river flowing through my rhythm, my poem, my rhyme... You are the lyrics that touch my sensibilities, my words spoken in sincerity. You are the perfect answer to my questions, and the reason for my tranquility. You are my forever love, my companion, my âme soeur, and my friend. It is you, my love, and only you. There is no one who I desire more...

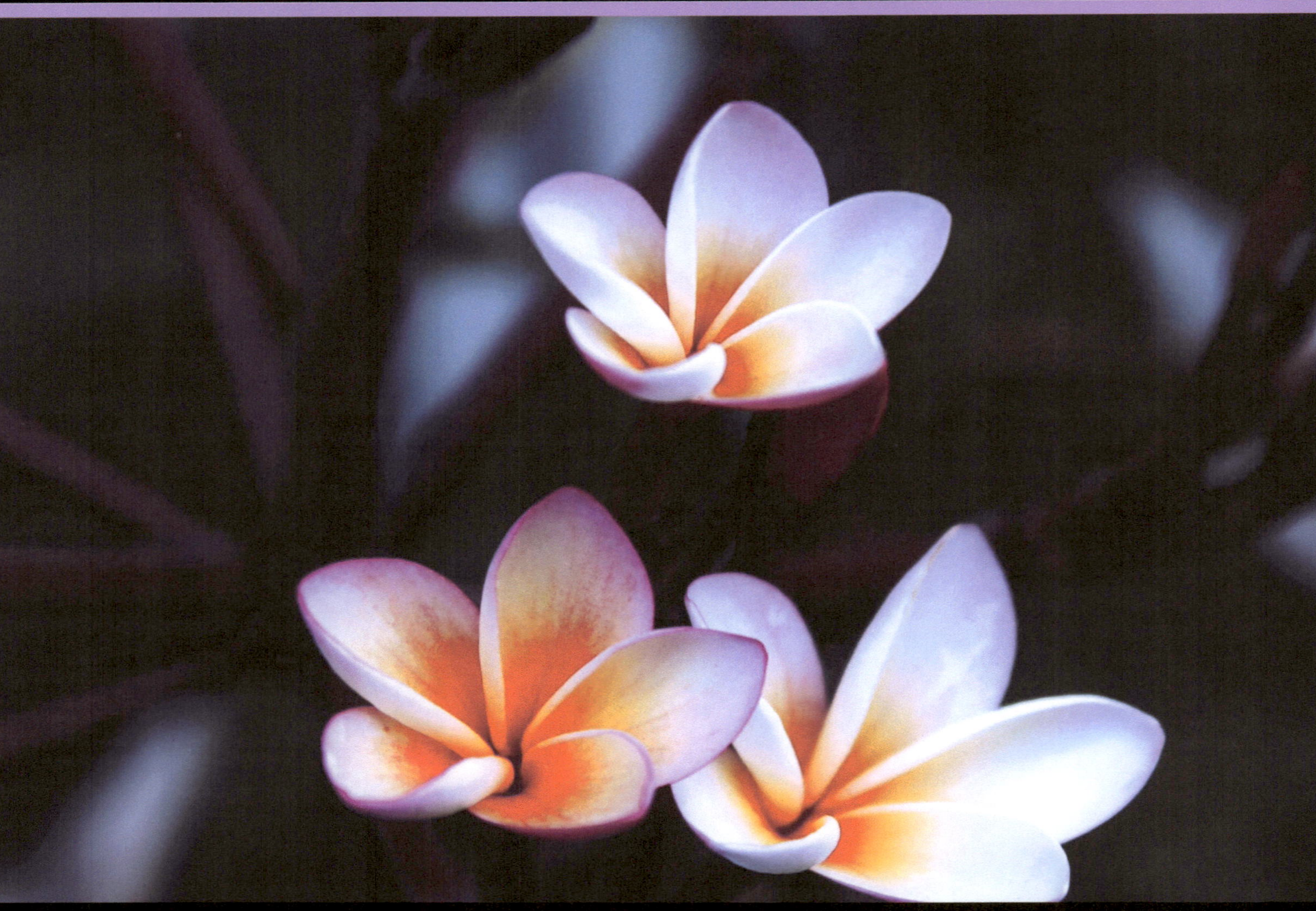

I cannot close my fist and say I love you, so my hands are opened wide... I cannot make demands upon you and say that my love is not a lie. You are free of my encumbrances, because I want to watch you thrive. You were born to choose your own destiny and I celebrate your life. I'll be your anchor and embrace your liberty, because true love cannot be contained and when you love, it is free...

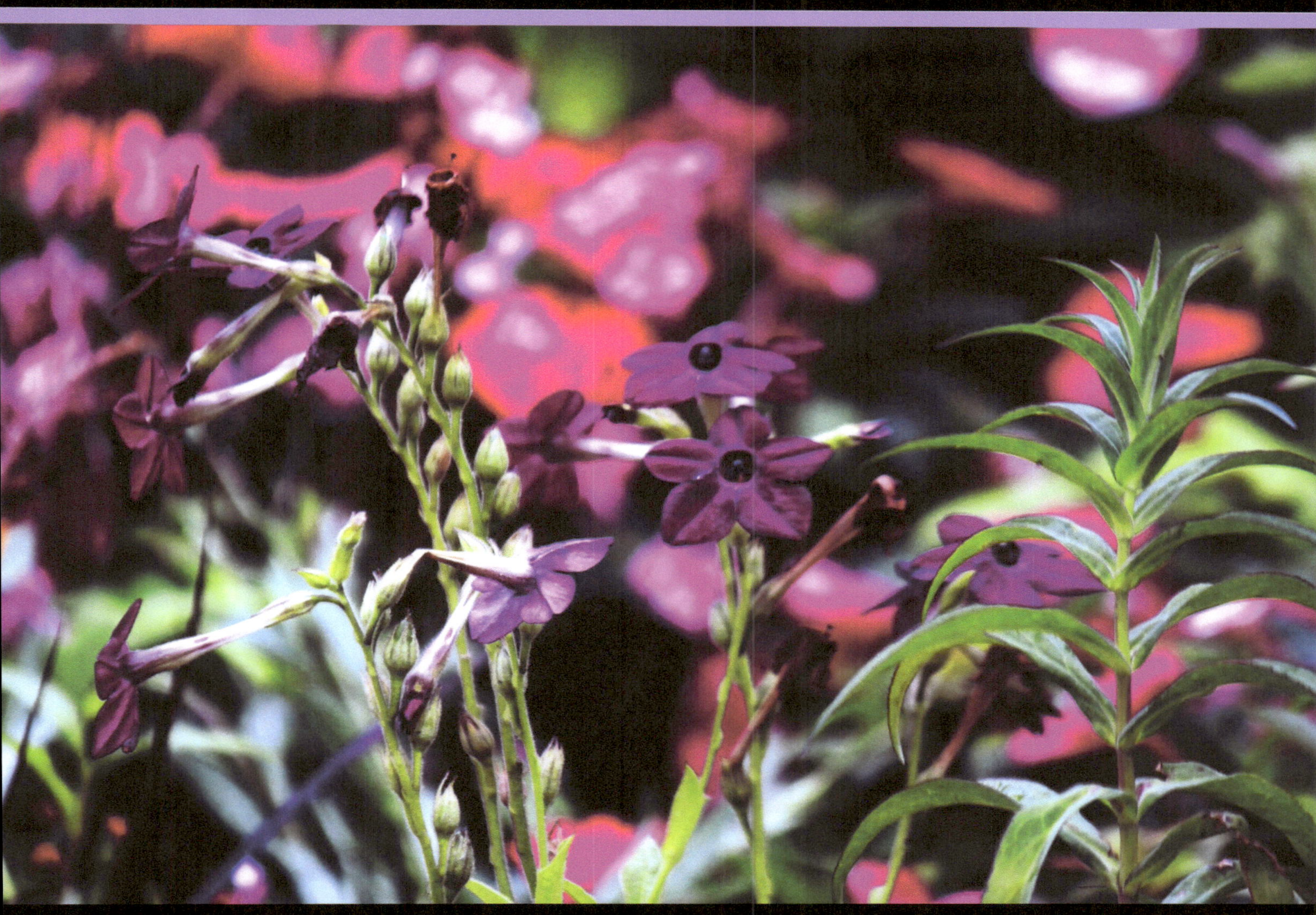

I love you unlike I have ever loved any one or anything in my life. What you have given me is so much more than mere words can explain. Your kindness lifts me higher, and with just the soft touch of your kiss, I soar into paradise. Just the thought of you brings a smile to my lips, and my heart trembles at the very sight of you. And when you laugh, I feel like joy is pouring over me, and I am made whole.

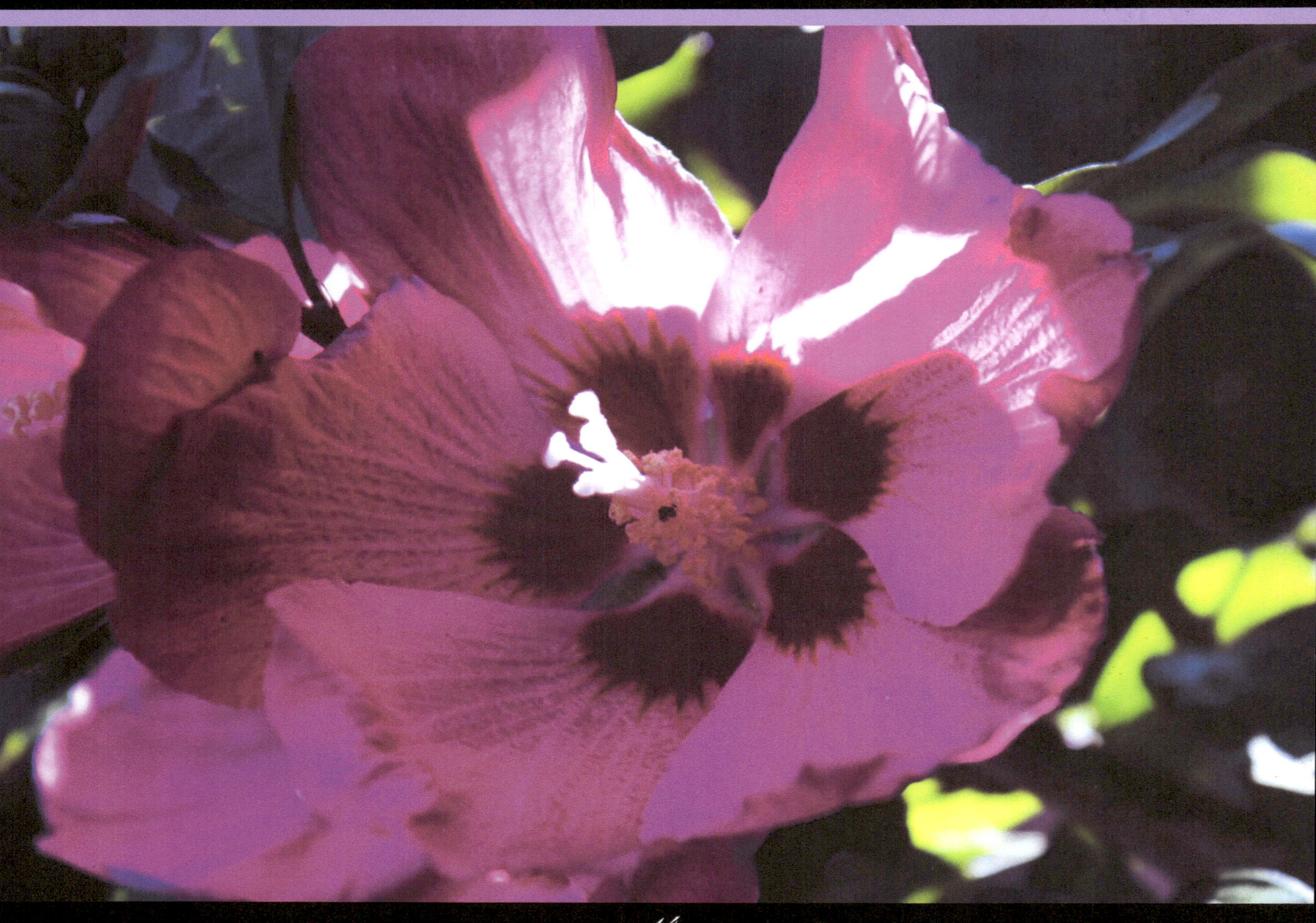

Because I love you, I can sing songs in harmony all by myself. And when you speak, I am moved to listen diligently, for your words, they bring me peace. I hear symphonies in your laughter; a melodic sonnet at the sound of your voice. I hear the echoes of angels praying each time you speak those three perfect words...I love you... And my melody hums to the beat of your heart because I am in love with you...

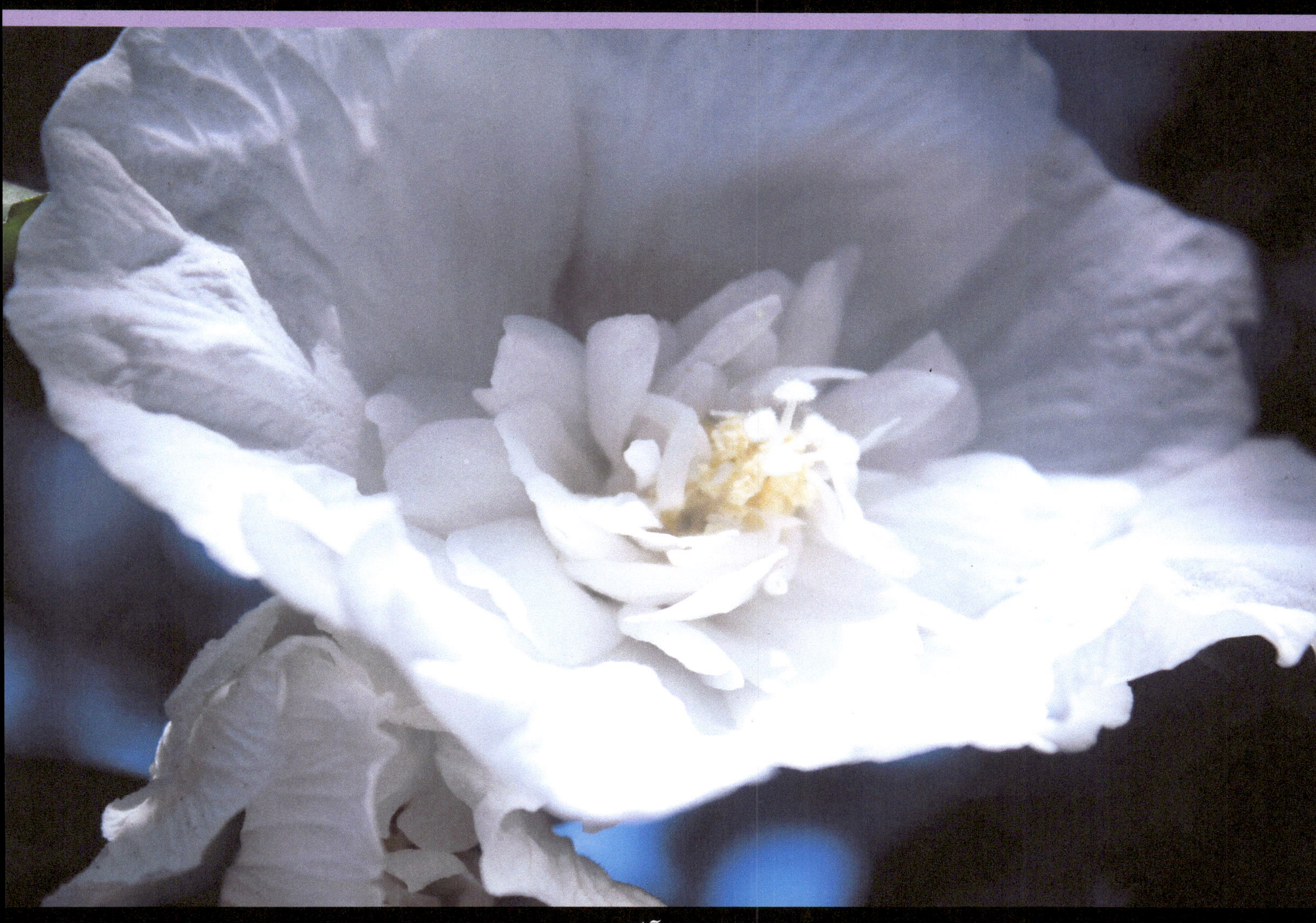

My Dearest Love... If you ever leave me, I'd be an orphan wandering aimlessly through the dark tepid world without a home. Oh, my love, you are my inspiration; the joy inside my soul. How could I ever be without you. You are the sole reason for my faith and the mirror of my smile. Love, make haste and embrace me, for when I'm in your arms I feel alive...

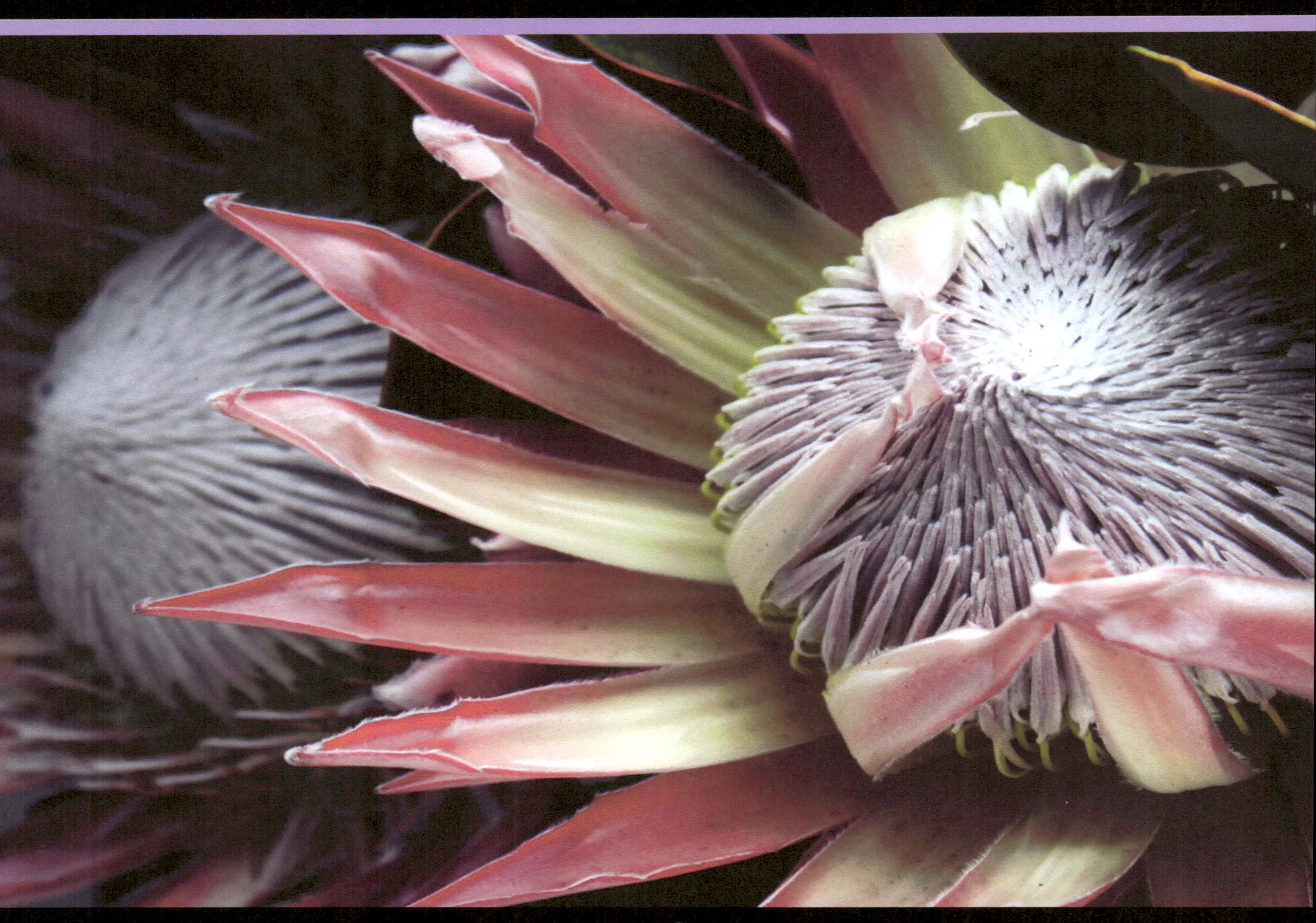

Pray for me...that I may reach the heavens where you lay your head. Comfort me...that I may rest in the gentle comfort of your wings. Hold me... Keep me close until eternity, until all darkness fades. Love me...that I will never feel lonely. Be my love, my one and only. Wrap me in the cradle of your sacred loving arms... Be my light through the tunnel. Be my angel for all time...

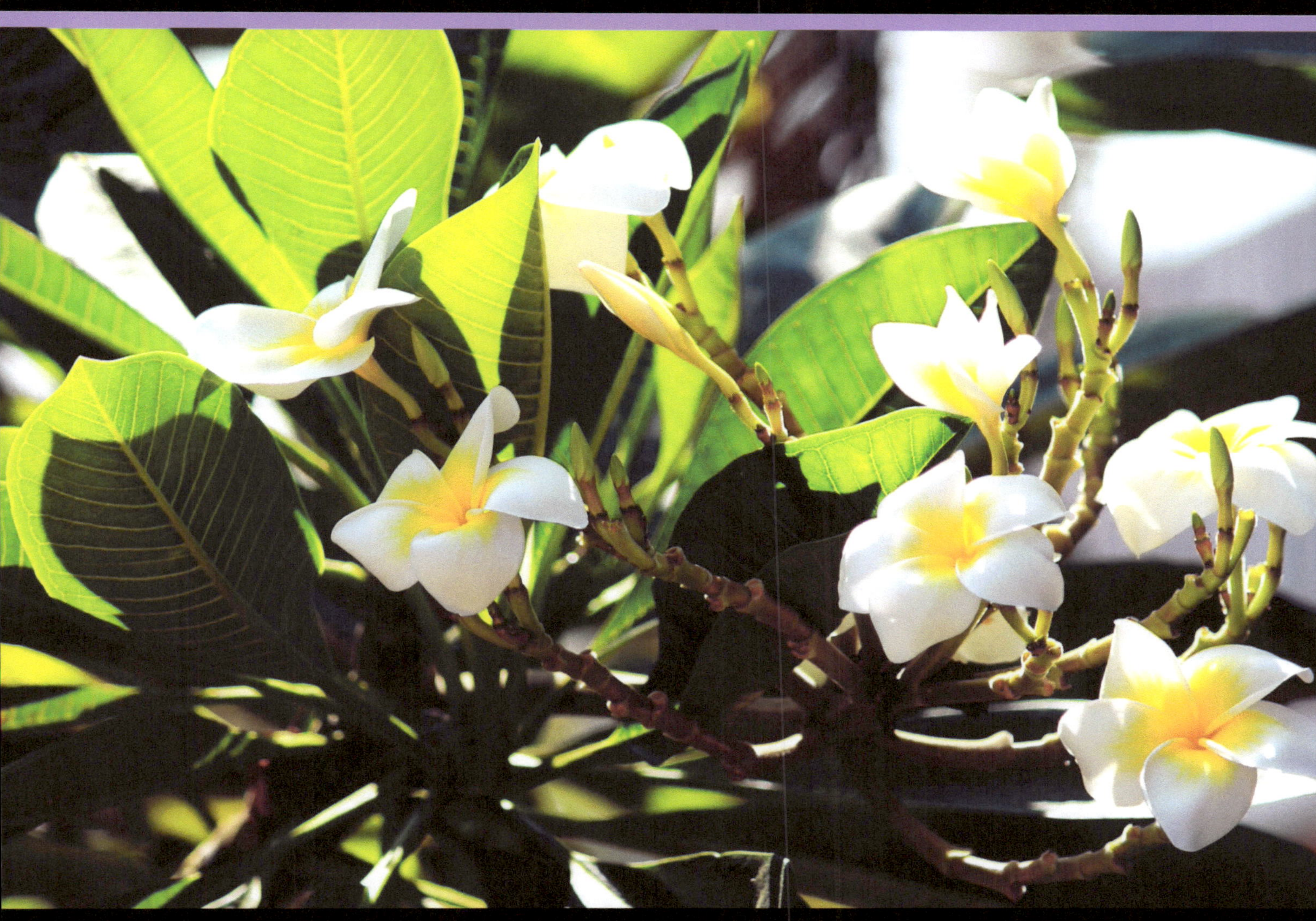

If these are my last words, then let me say them from the profoundest depths of my heart. You have been my resurrection in times of trouble and my joy in my days of mirth. And I shall laugh with you forever and always throughout all time and space. For you are my everlasting love and neither absence nor death shall ever take it away. My soul journeys through paradise with each and every moment that I love you...

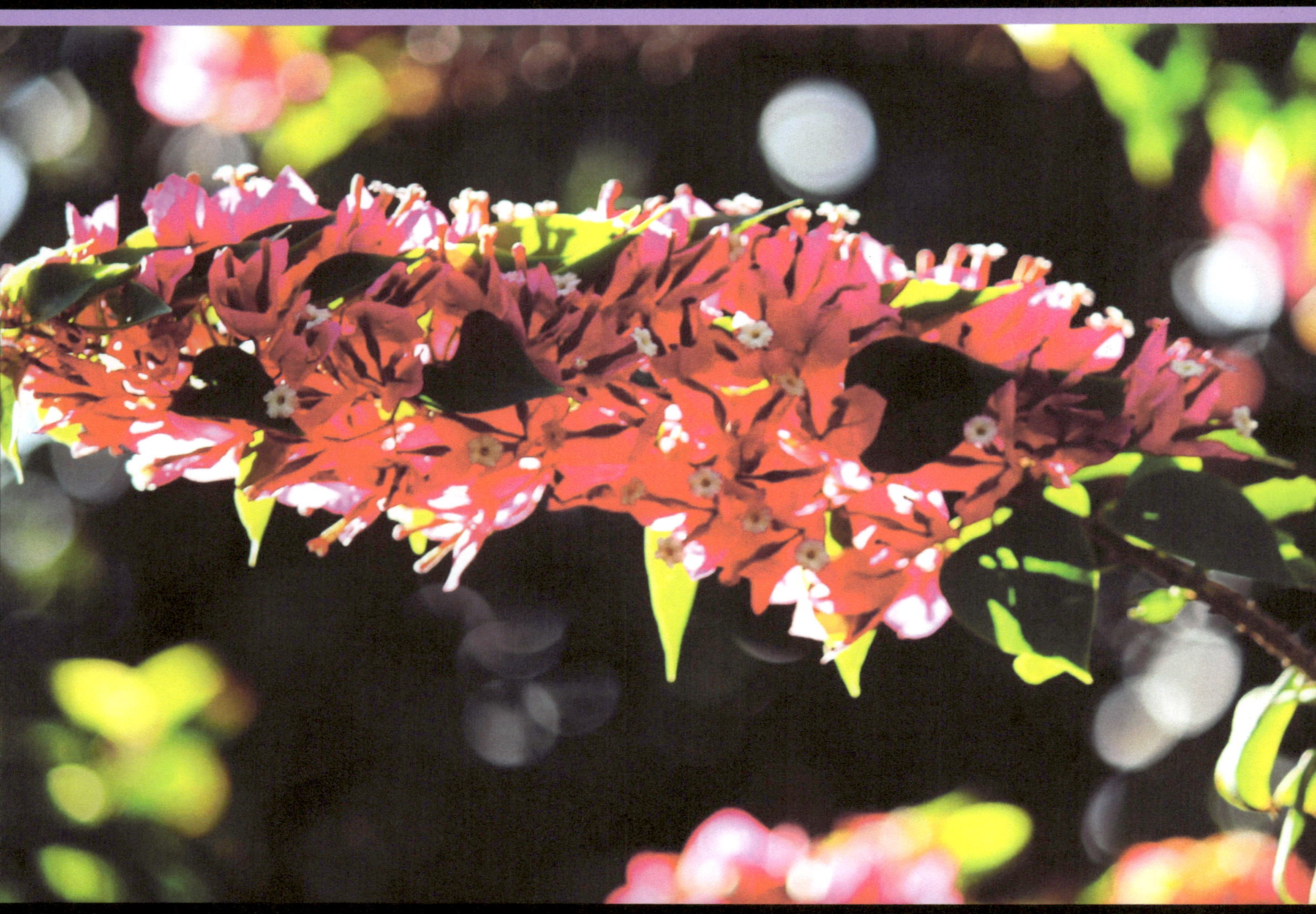

Look in my eyes... What I feel for you is real. Feel my heart beating... Don't you know how much I care about you? Let us be without the doubts that cause us pain. Let us love... Believe that our bond is meant to be. We were meant to enjoy the desire we feel. Let us live... We were ordained to be happy together. Love is our most precious gift and we were born to partake of it forever...

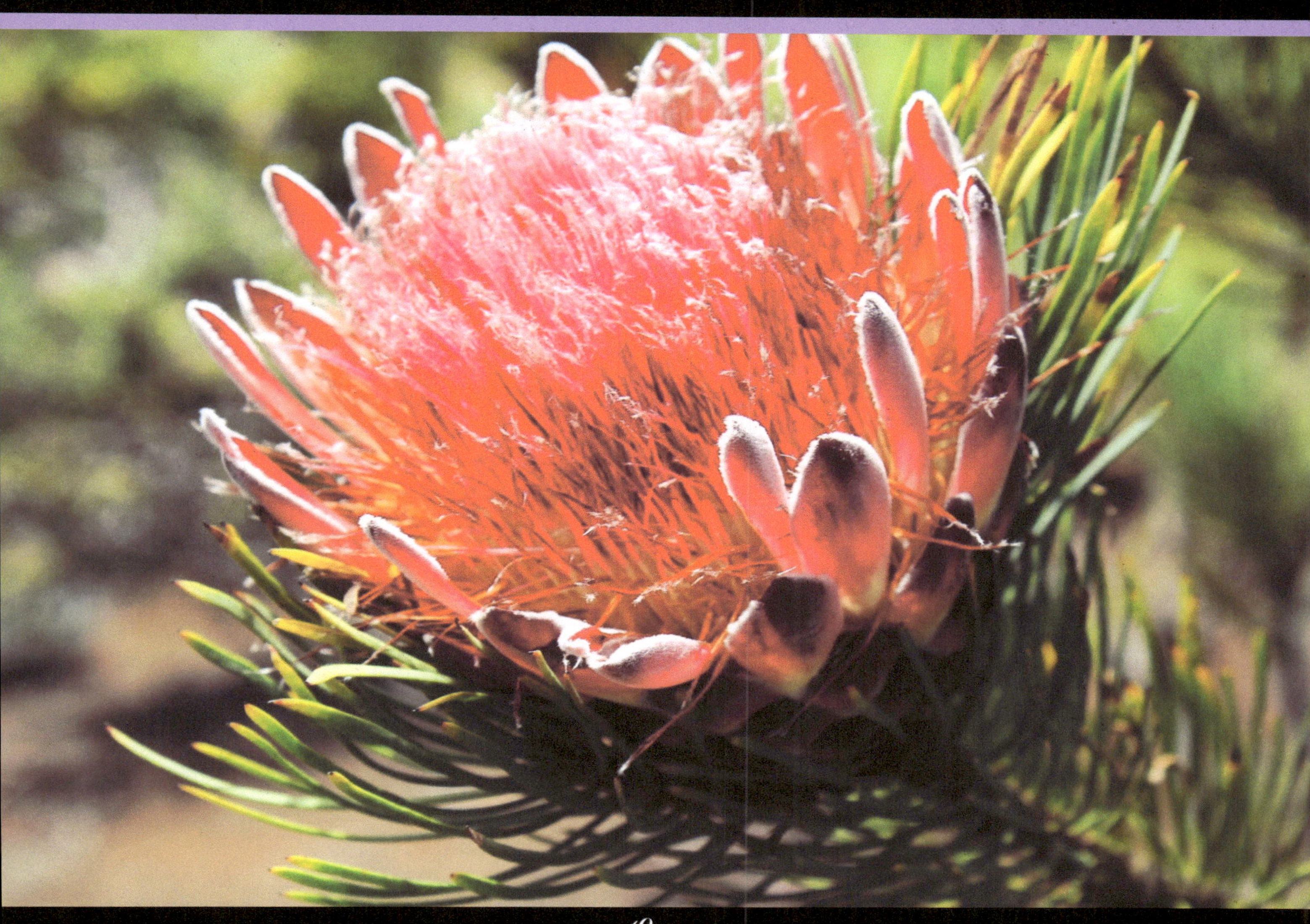

I am sorry... I am weak. Nothing about me is perfection. I am fallible. I have run out excuses. If I could unspeak my words... If I could unbreak your trust... What I would give to undo my deeds and unlove my false lovers... If I could love you again; hold you again, I would love you with no reason for regret... And I would you love with all my heart...

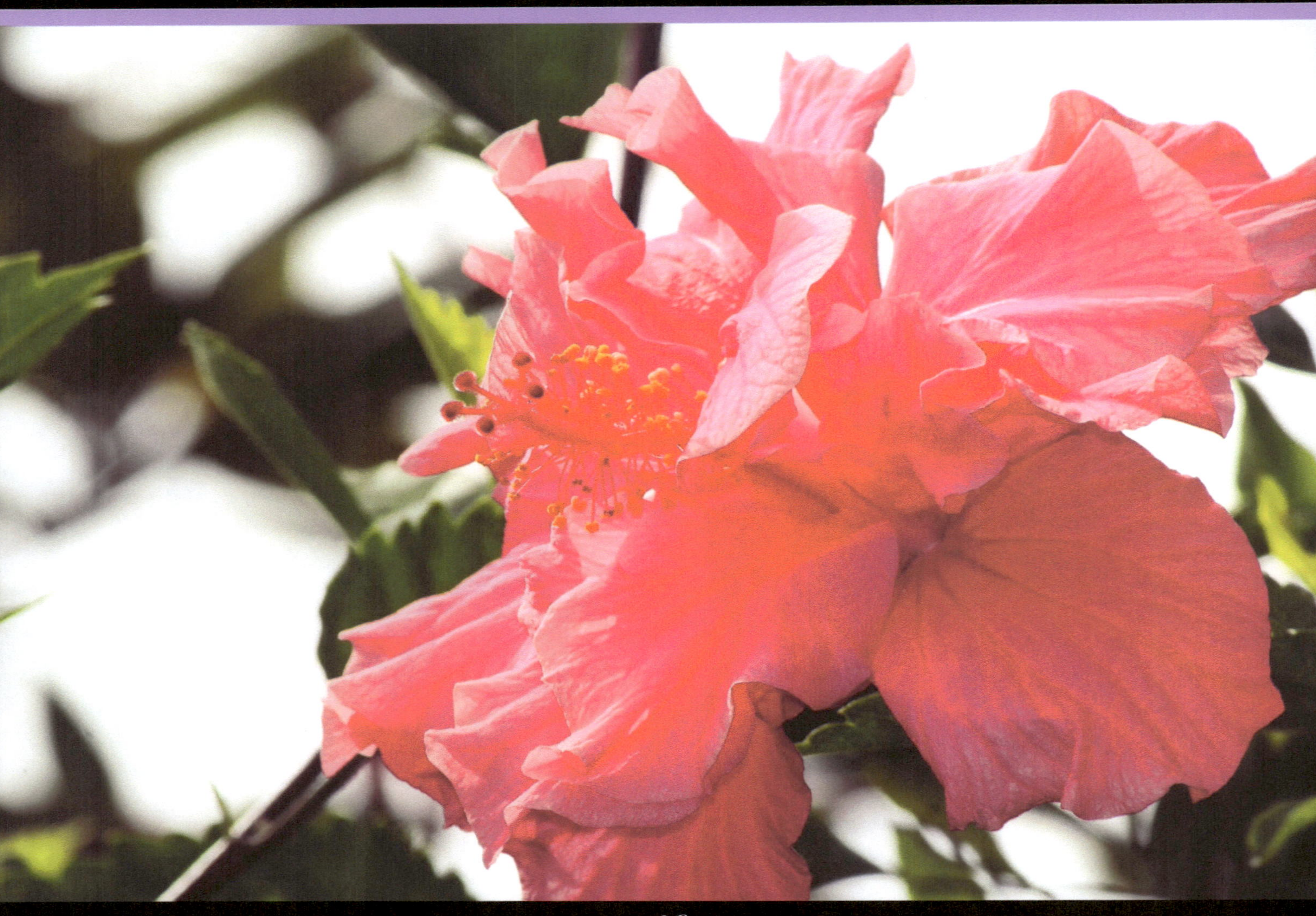

Oh, how beautiful you are. Oh, how lovely is your smile... You have enchanted me with your heart and I can't contain my joy. My darling, you give me someone to love; someone to adore. And each day that I'm with you, my life is filled with love. I am so happy to be with you and faithfully in yours arms. There is no greater gift than the grace God has given me in just one day of loving you...

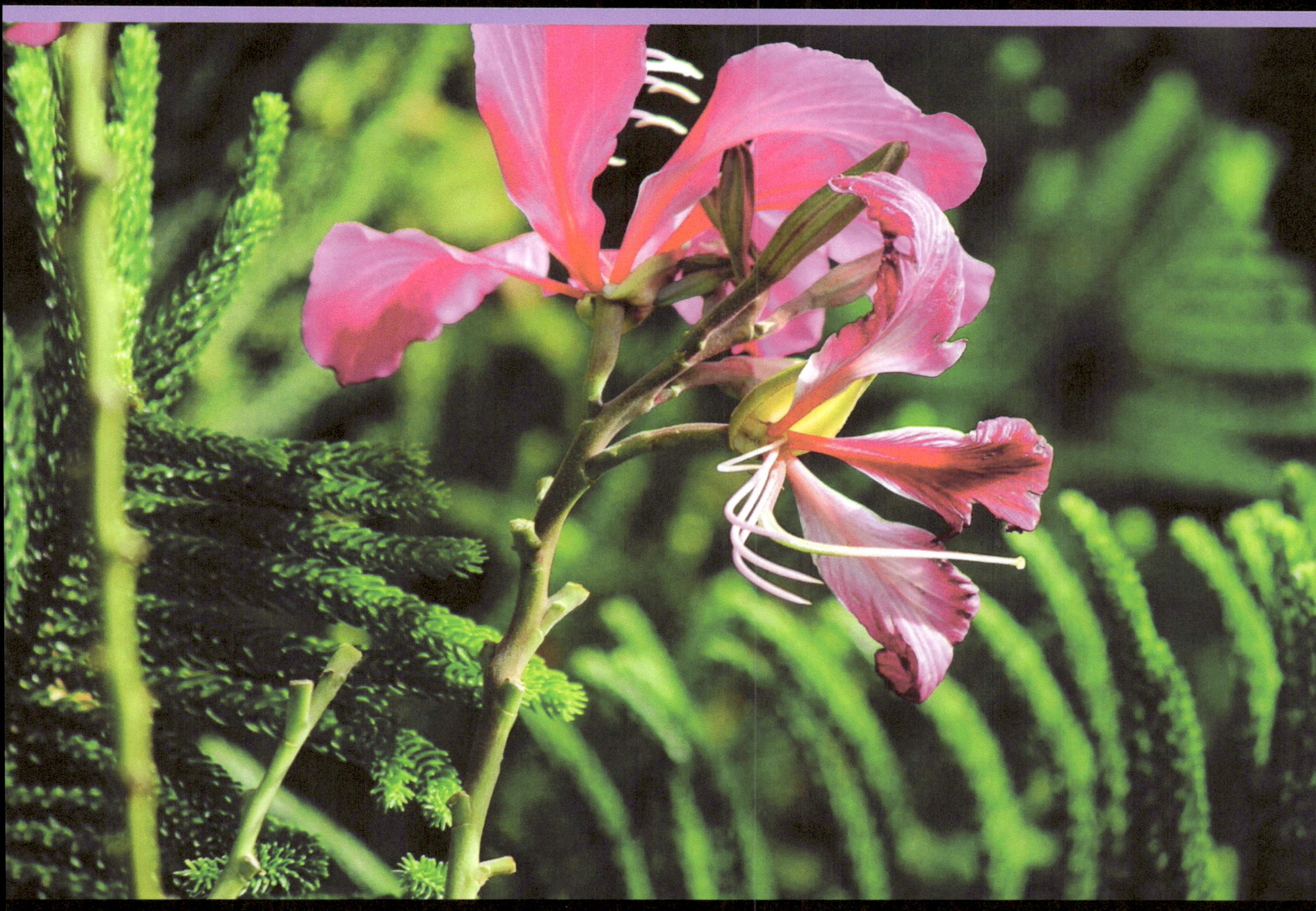

Your love consumes me, yet jealousy ruins me. I'm drowning in the depths of insecurity. Why must I be so thin-skinned. My mind fills conjures up with places where you've never been? Is it my fear that I'm unworthy of being your love or am I just afraid of losing you to someone? Will you find another more worthy than me? No... It doesn't matter...because true love is free...

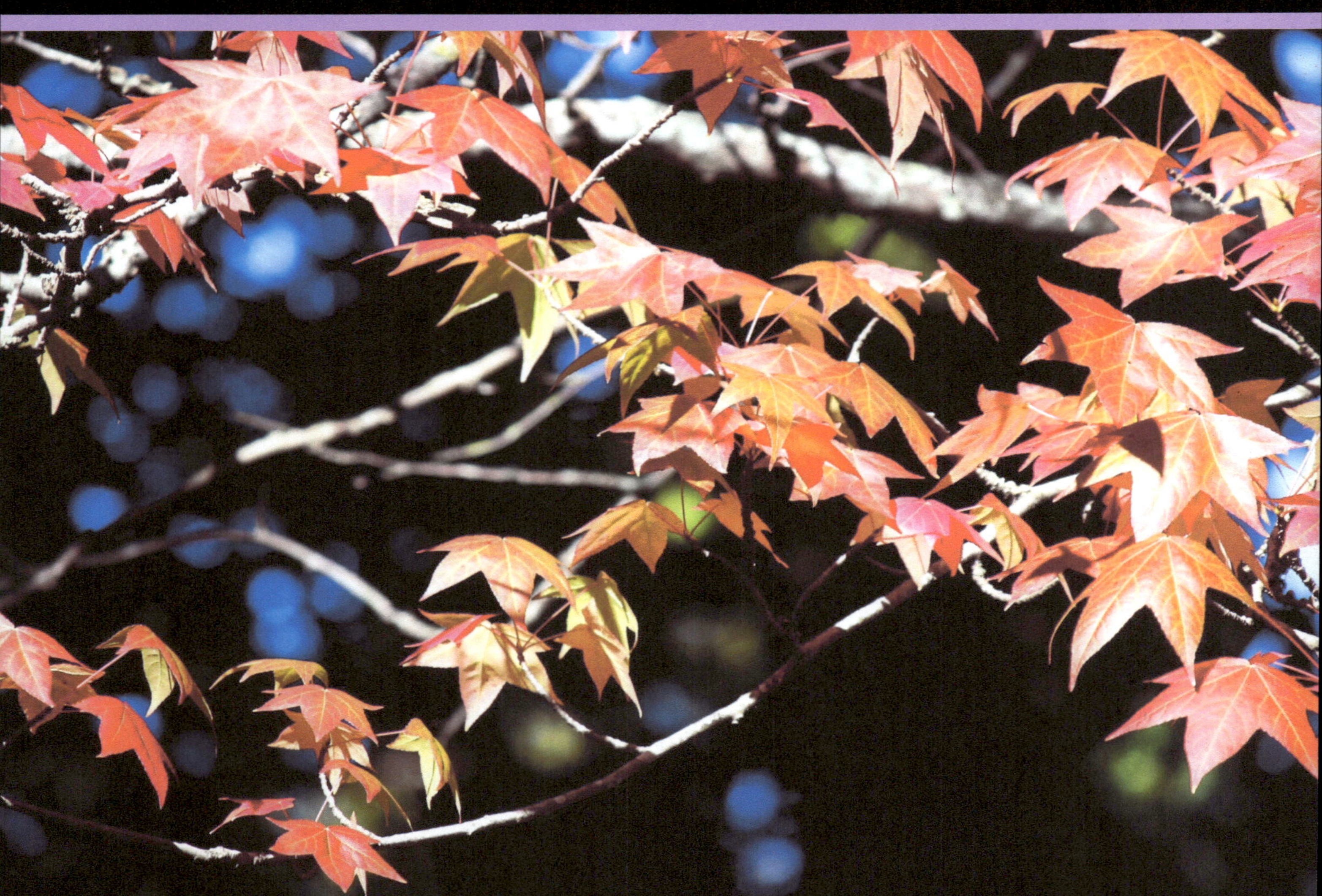

Come... Lay your head next to mine. My arms are opened wide. I will unburden you of your troubles. You have nothing to hide. I will carry you on my shoulders and lift you up above the crowd. I am standing right here with you and I will never leave your side... I will never leave you lonely, when you're hurt, or in need. You are an integral part of me... And I love you, no matter where life leads...

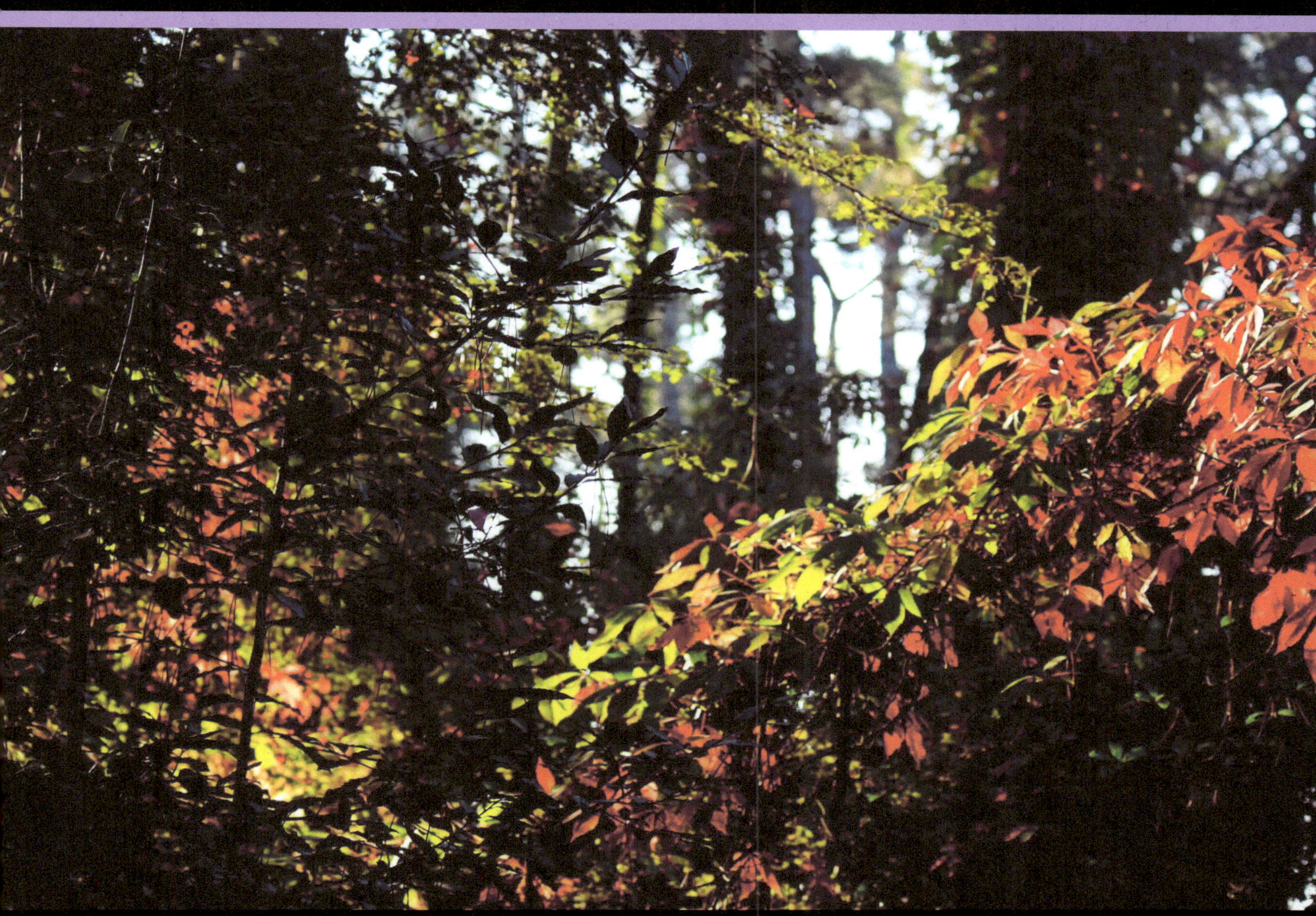

Let's lie down in a forest pure; a place where love is refined. We'll run through the thickets of I don't care and wallow in the grass of the sublime. I'll be your protector through the wild, wicked delightful world. I'll be the one who you can depend on. I'll be the one that you'll love. Take my hand and we'll walk together... You'll never regret your hand is in mine, for our life is lived in precious moments; now and through all time...

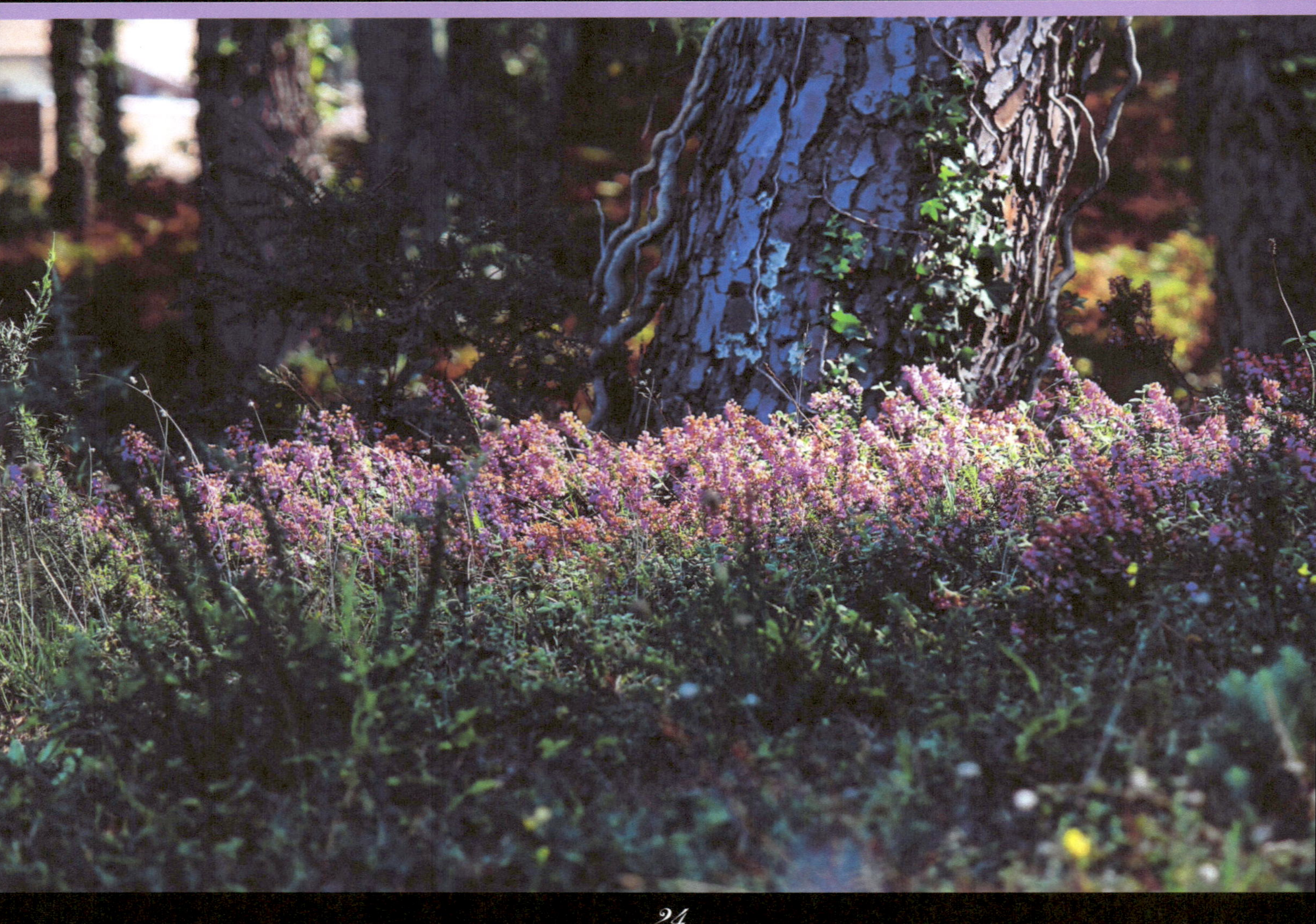

Fine wine... Black cherries... That is what you are... Lovely as summer's eve under the moonlit sky. You are beautiful from your heart to your soul. And I want to taste you with my tongue of love. You taste like ripe berries dipped in delicious cream. I can't help drinking your kisses. I'm drunk from your skin. Let me explore you further in my love nest. I have a place just for us; let's make haste it's getting late.

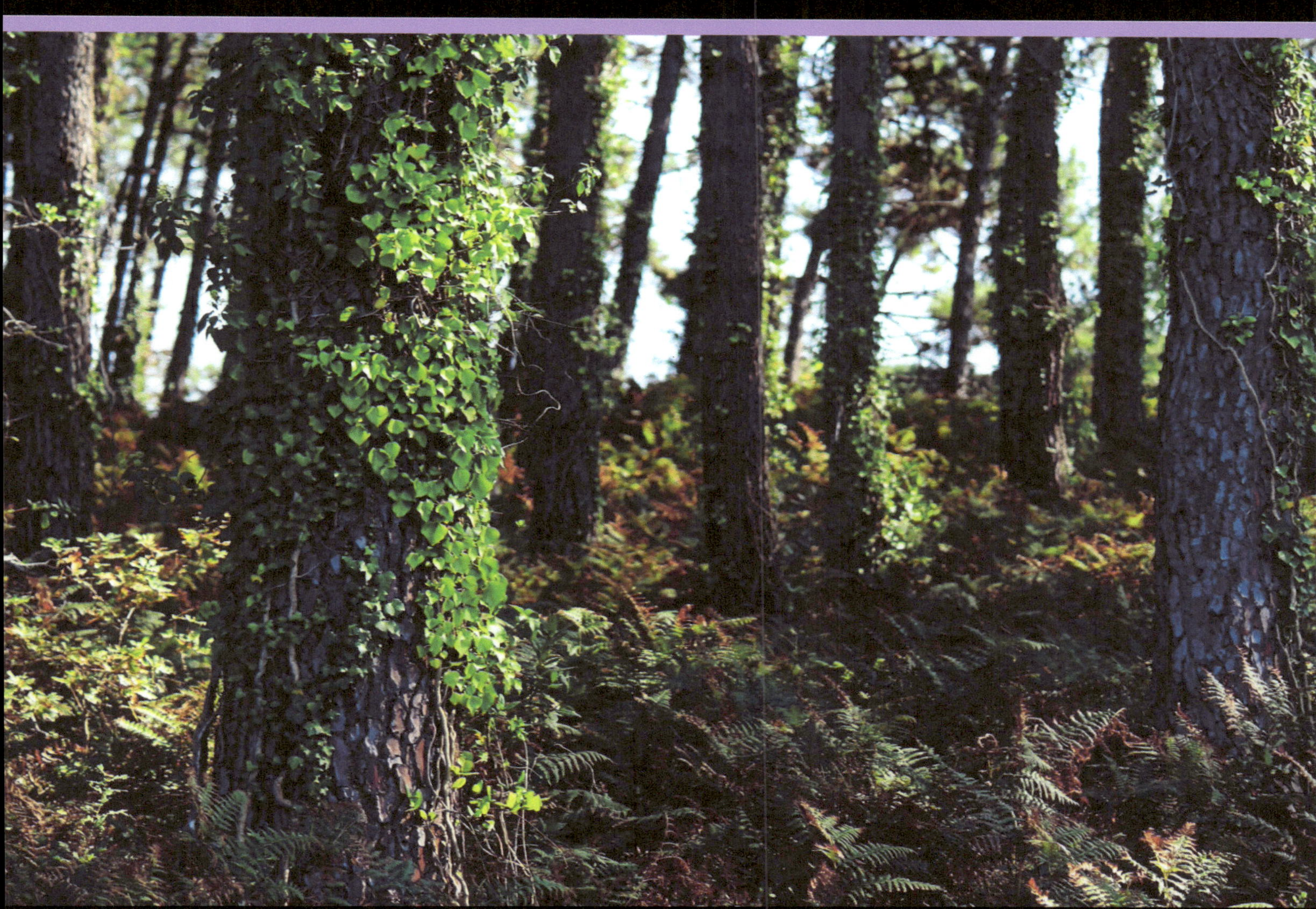

Dance with me.... Melt into the curves of my form. Move with me... Like the music of a tango swaying in harmony, back and forth. Make love with me...like the wind in the trees and the butterflies among the leaves. Marry me.... Be my love, my one and only, and our joy shall surely be if you would only... Marry me...

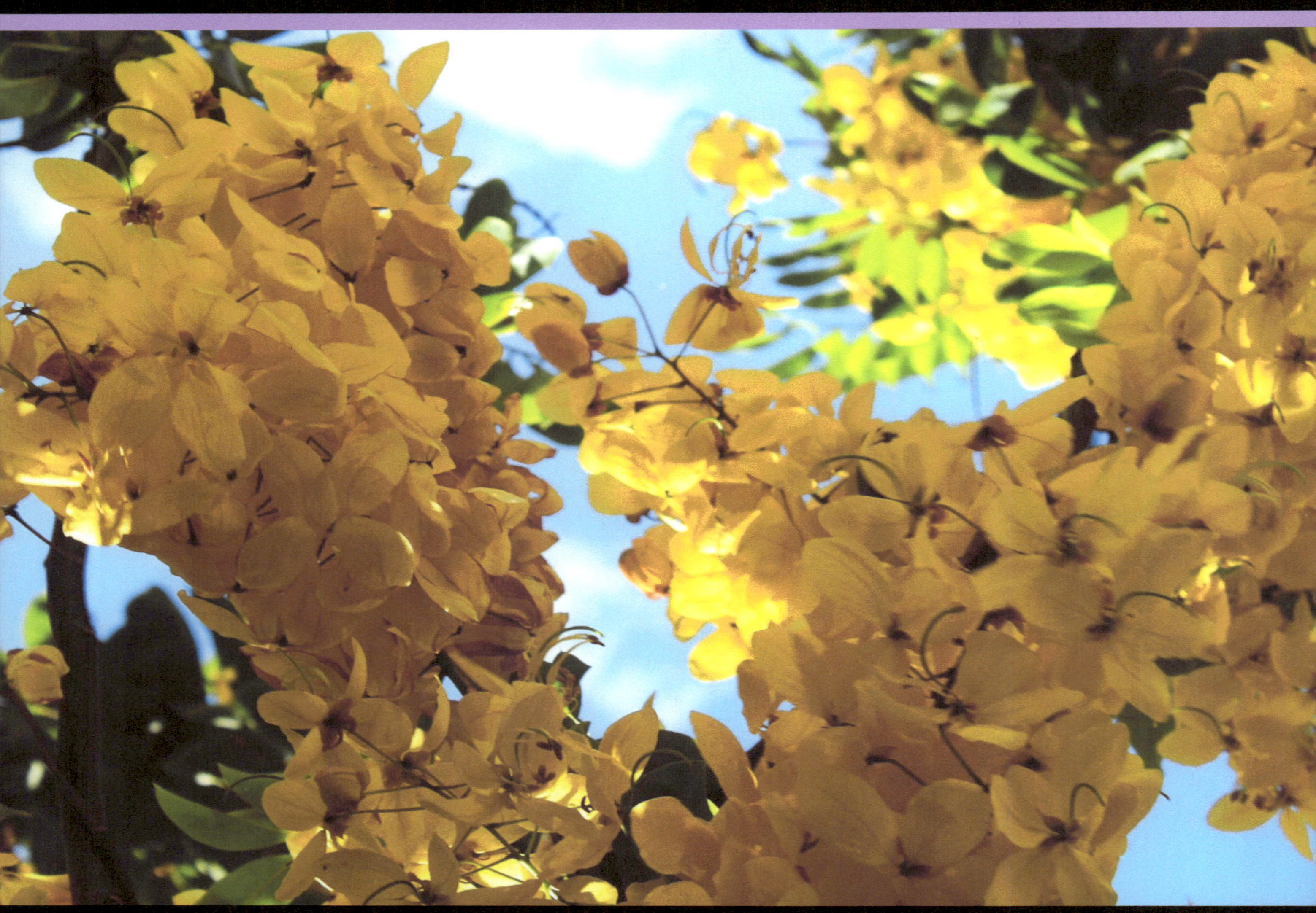

If there was one thing that you would demand of me, what would it be? Would you ask for me to change my ways, my profoundest dreams, my friends, or even my life? Would you wish for me to change my dress, my hair, go away with you, or travel here or there? Well, I will seek to fulfill your wishes for they are my command. But if you ask me to love you less? I can't... My heart is in your hand...

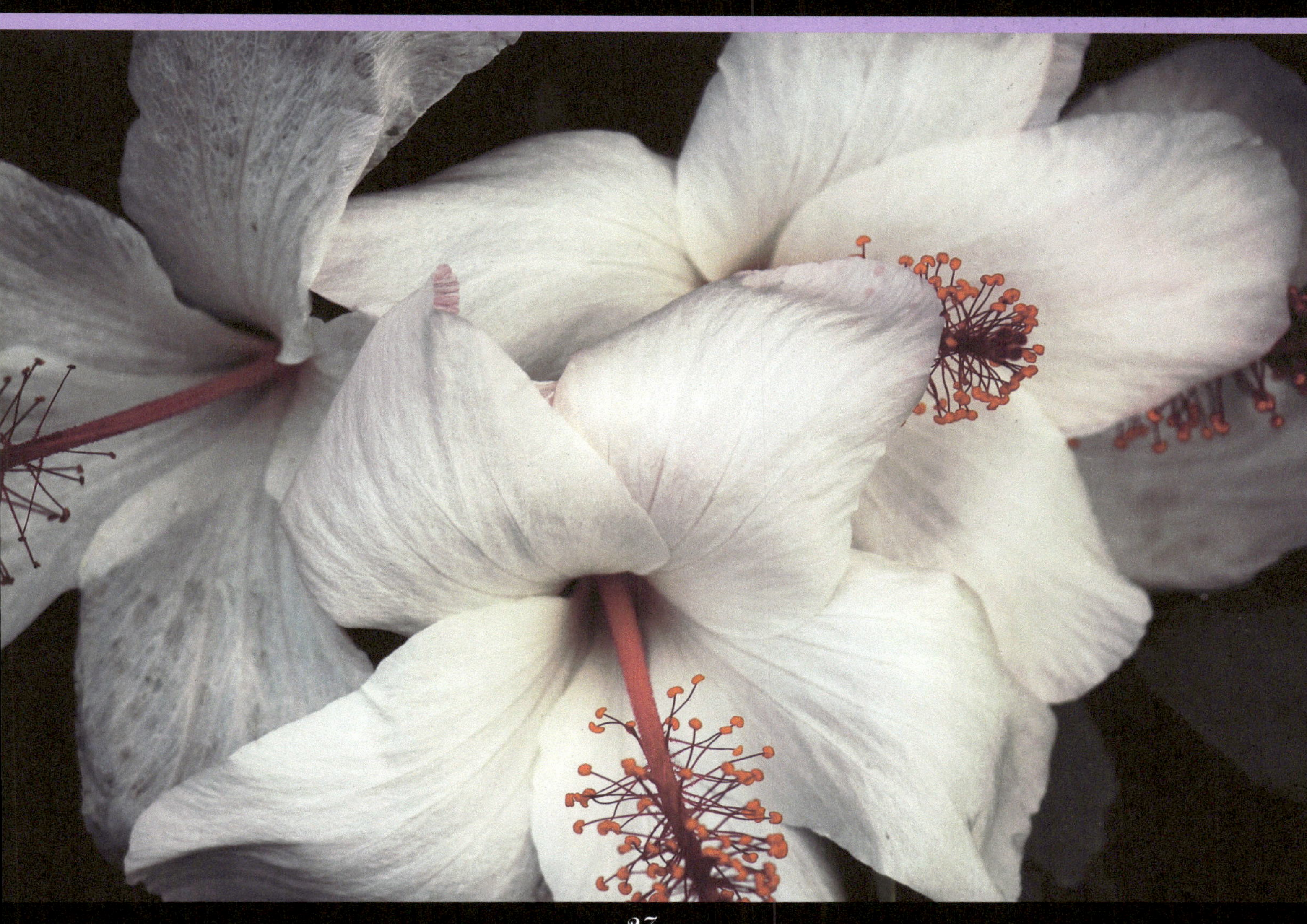

If I ever do something to hurt you, or reproach you when you only merit my love... Or if I ever dare to insult you when you deserve nothing less than the kindest words in the world... And if I error in my misunderstanding and my confusion cause you to recluse, I beg you to forgive me... Pardon me, my darling, for you are more precious than my imperfections. And I humbly honor you and kneel before you, and I ask your forgiveness now.

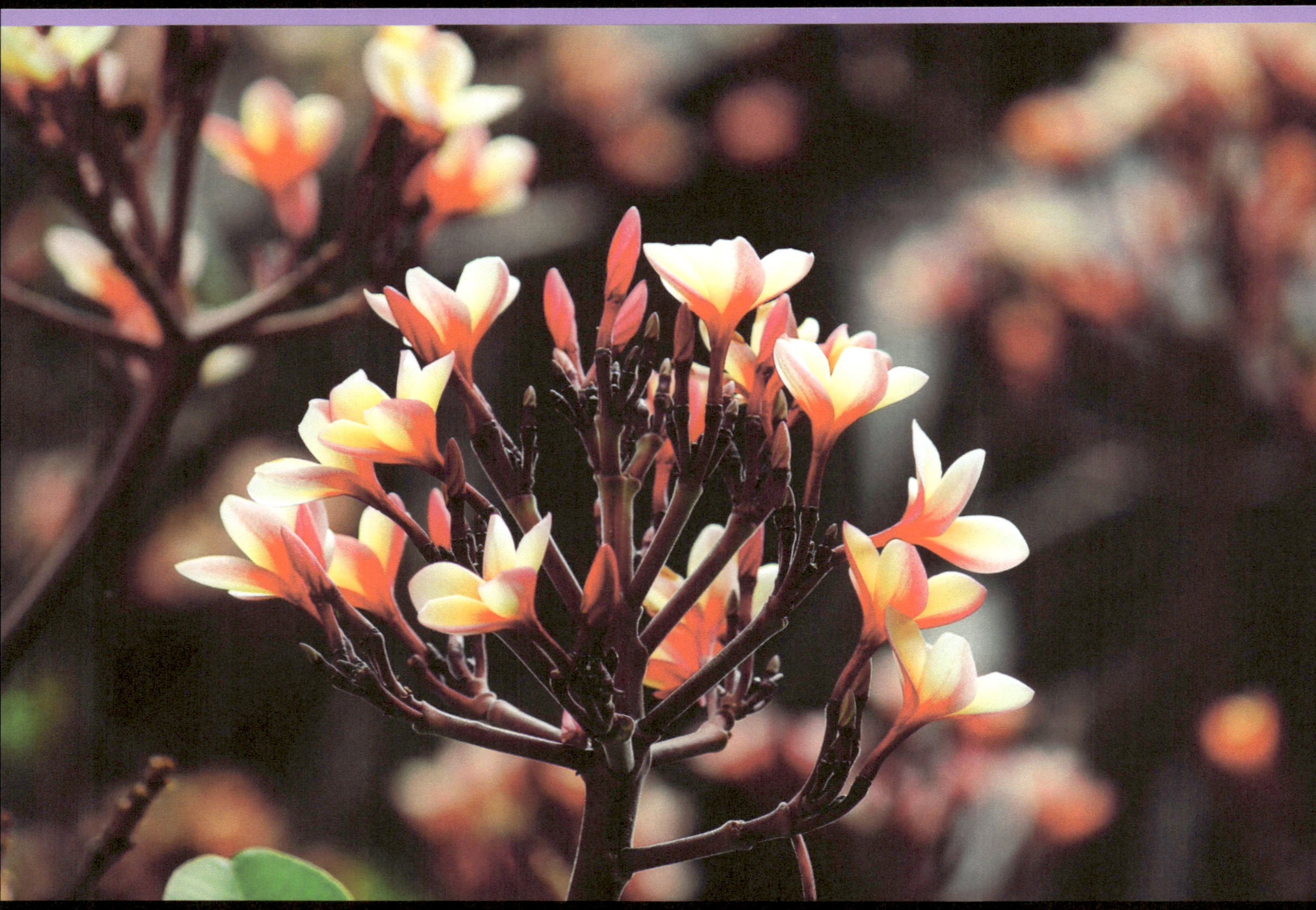

There is no one I would rather walk this life with than you. It's not just because we know how to laugh even when we stumble and fall. It's not just because you raise me with your kind words, as you offer to lift me with your hand. It's not simply because you are joyous to be around. It's because you make my journey worth walking; you make me more than a better person and human being, you make me glad that I was born.

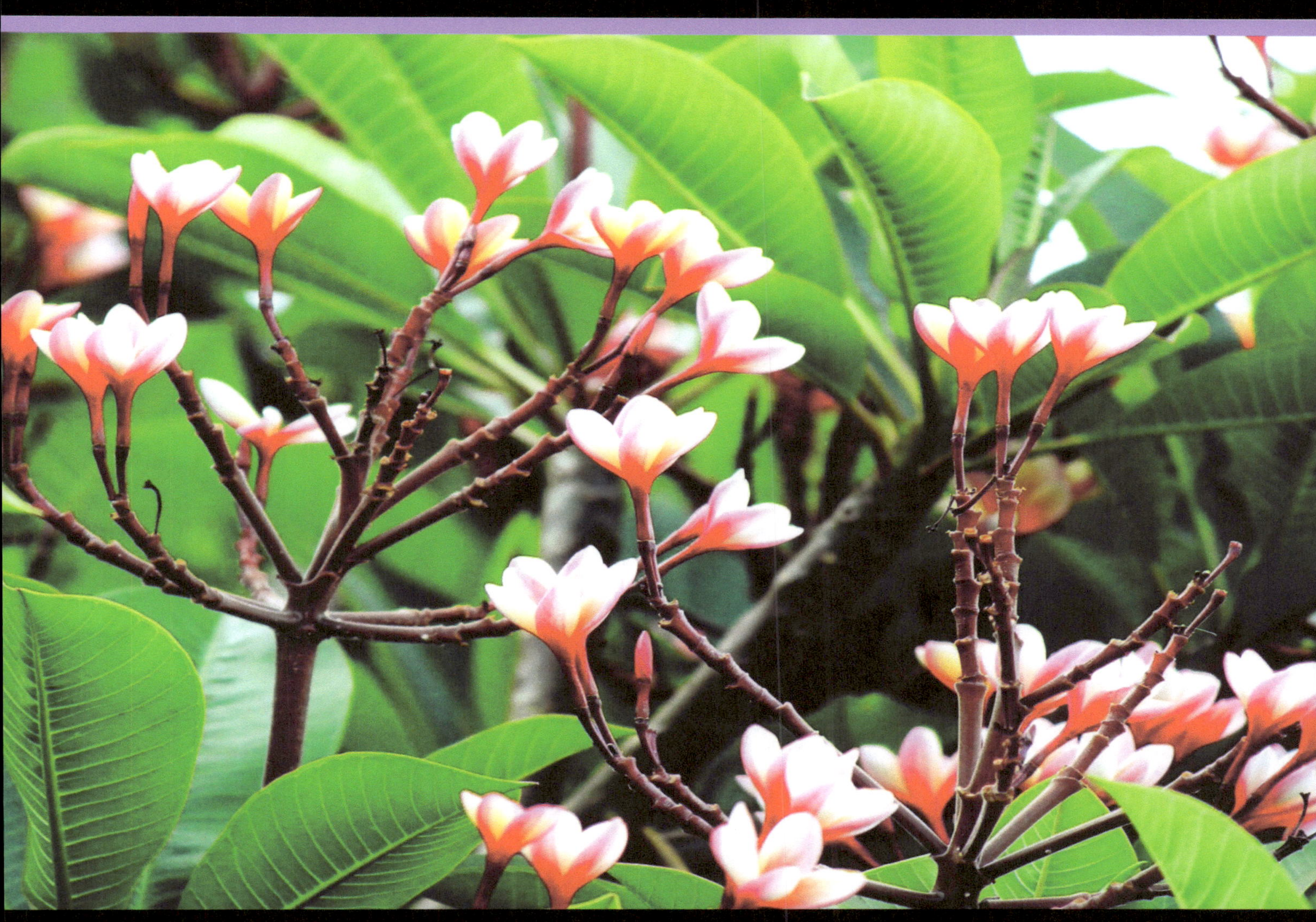

My Dearest Love... One kiss from your lips takes me to paradise. You move me with your softness... your sweet loving tenderness. You calm me with your gentleness of your voice and tell me kindly what I need to hear. And I listen, as I listen to the rain softly landing on my door, and you reassure me. Your love take my worries away. Your words are as sweet as the tender rain, and I am warmed by the hope in your heart.

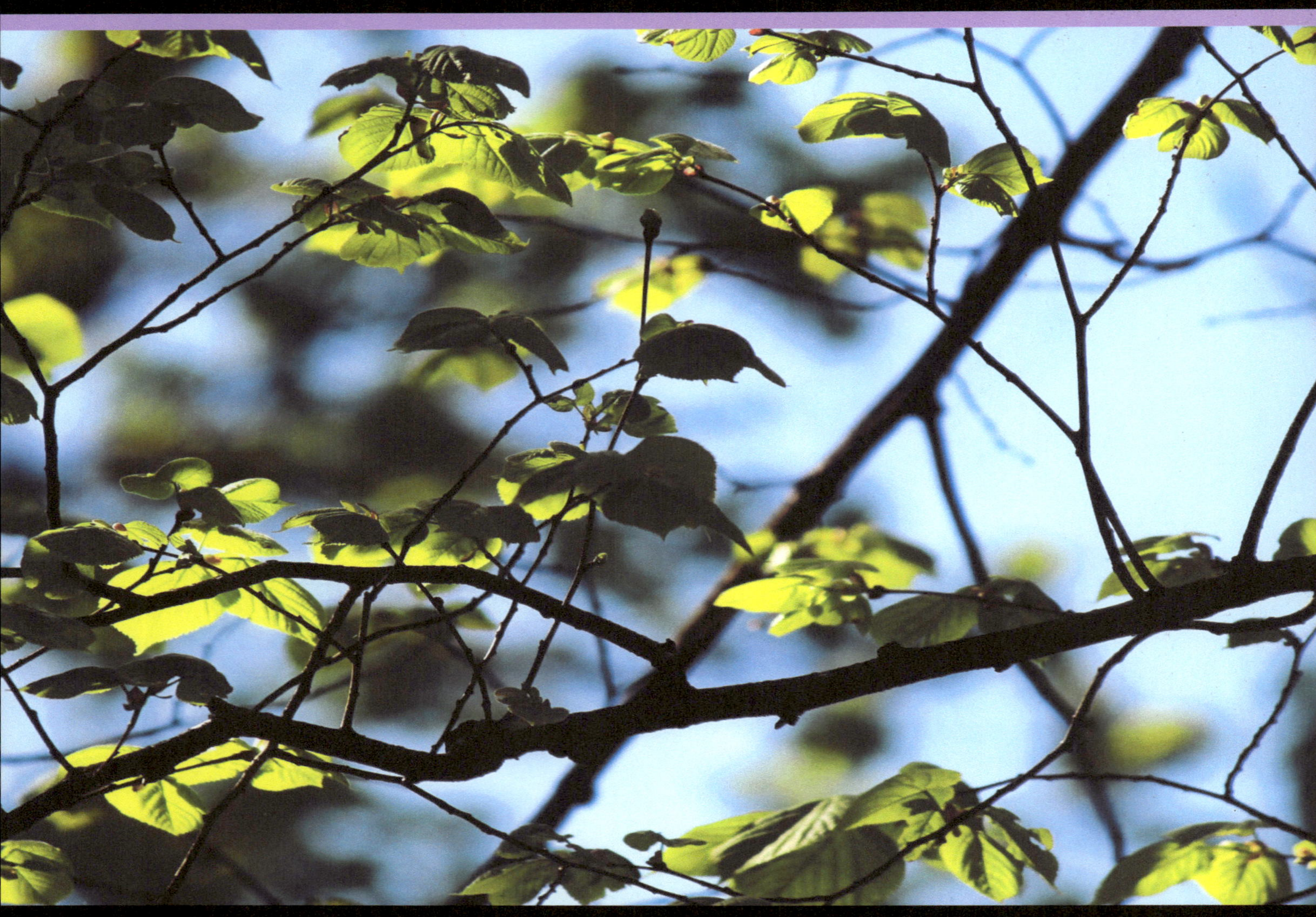

Beloved... why are you so sad? I have given you my heart. Lift your head and smile...for all I have is yours. I want to give the best of me, though my only good is in loving you. Do you need me to say those three words? Let me show you my love spoken in silence. Let me hold you close to me...Feel my devotion... Sense my my body next to you truth. Hear my heart saying, I love you... Let me make love to you...

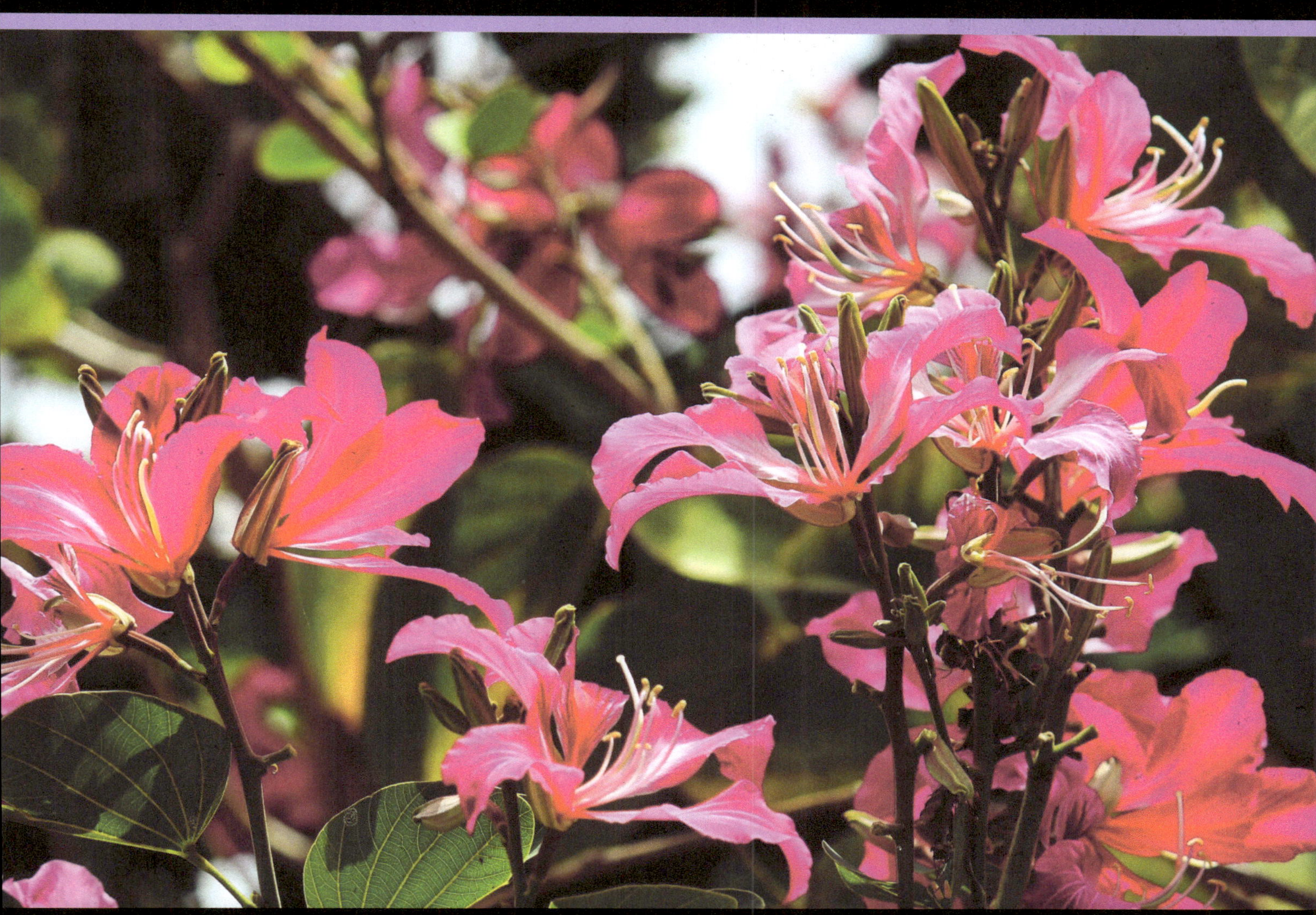

My funny Valentine... If you only knew how you affect me with your love. You pull me into your bliss. Your smile beams inside my heart. It's like a ray of sun shining on a lonely, lonely night. Oh, the joy I have since you've come into my life. What a lovely beautiful love we share, and it's all because of your smile...

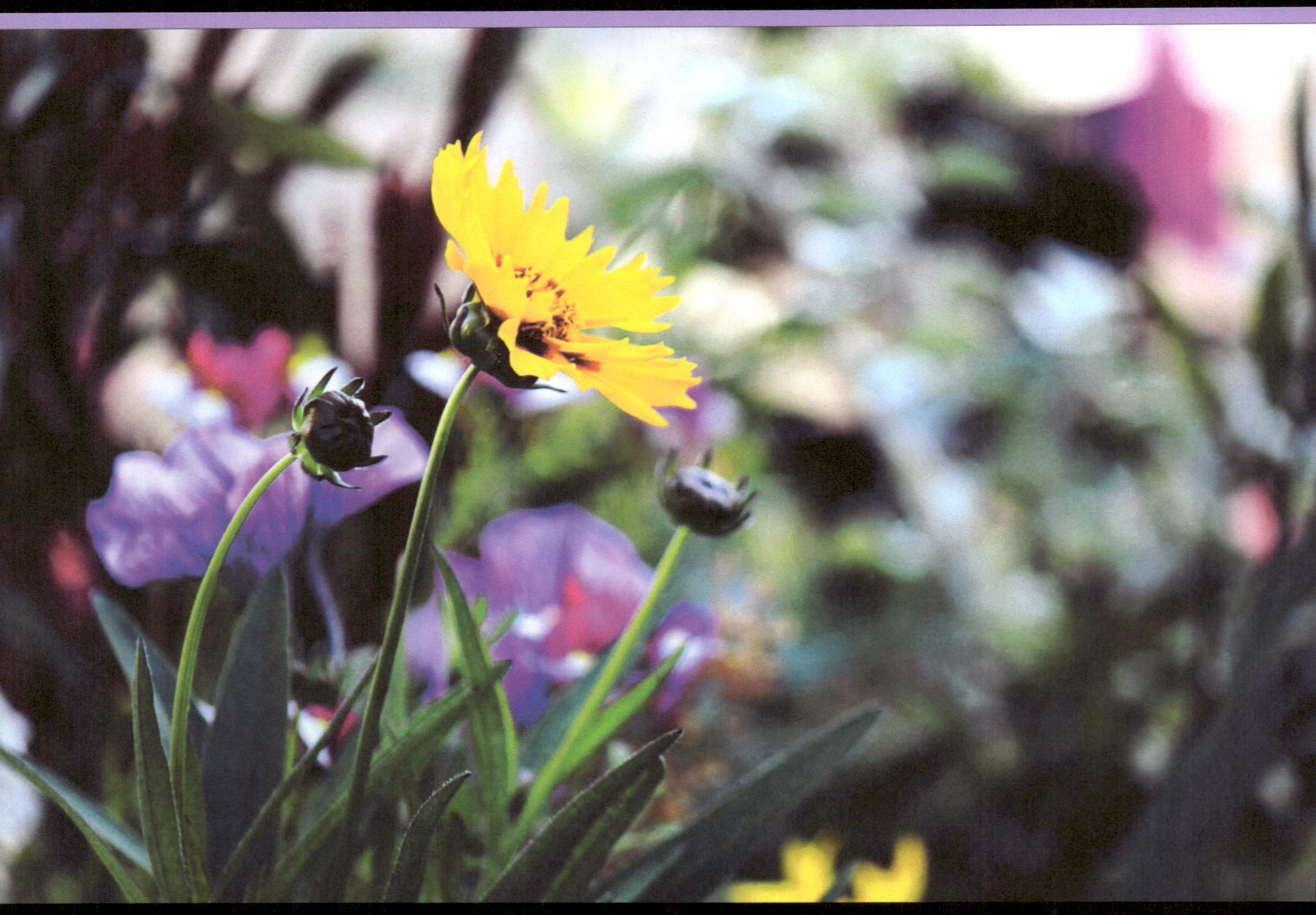

My love... My darling... You are so rare and wonderful; gorgeous to the eyes... Solid and reassuring... You make me weep with your touch. Do not be alarmed... For your magnificence overwhelms me, and I say what I feel without biting my tongue. You are remarkable, marvelous, and I am in love...

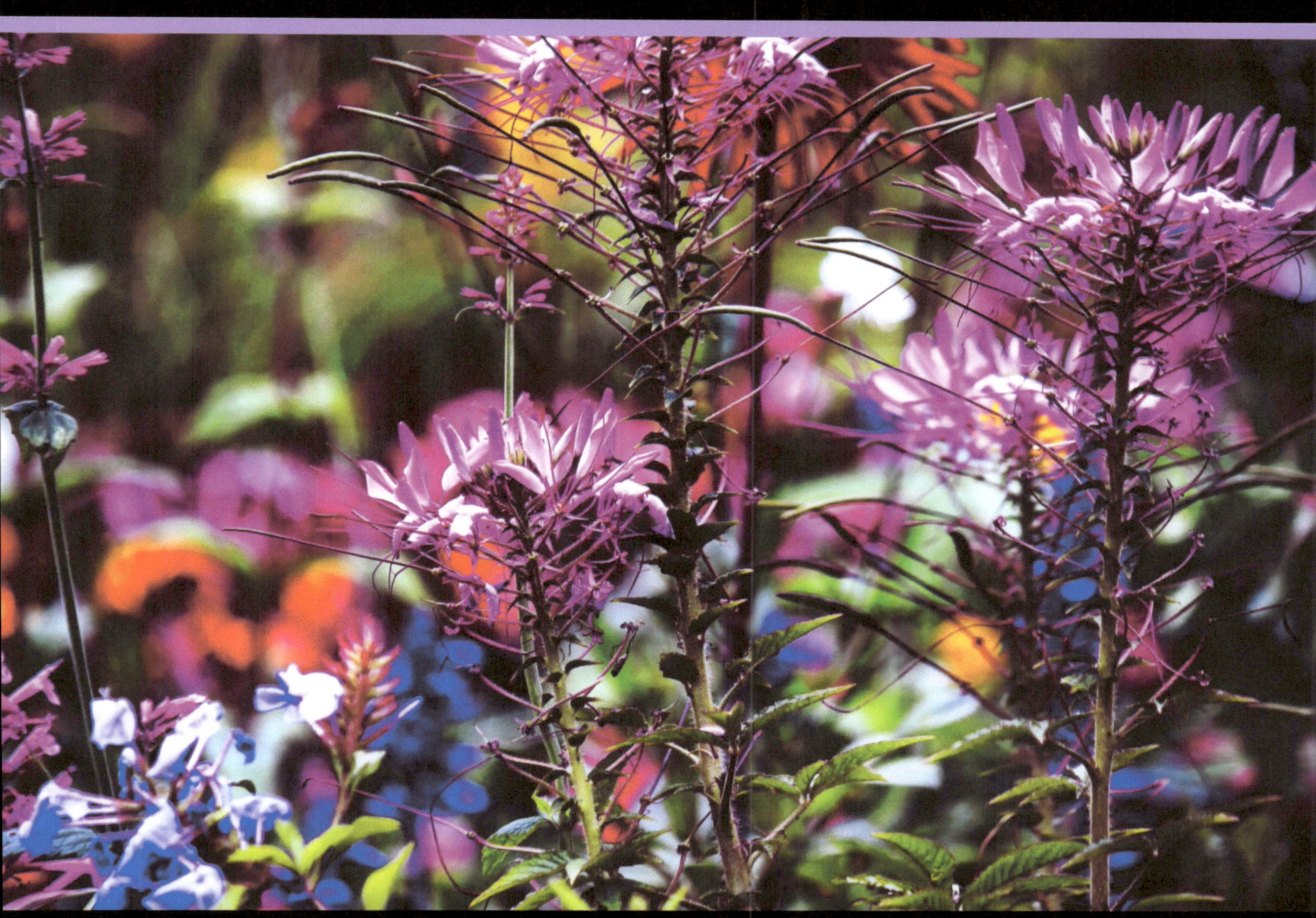

I could beg you to love me and I could beg you to stay, but love is freely given. Love cannot hold what does not wish to be kept, and we do not own what is heaven sent. I wish for your life to be blessed every day. Be wise in your journey and know that I am just a call away. Reach and achieve your goals, and keep me in your heart. I stand with you, whether you are near or very far. Always be true to who you are. You are my love forever...

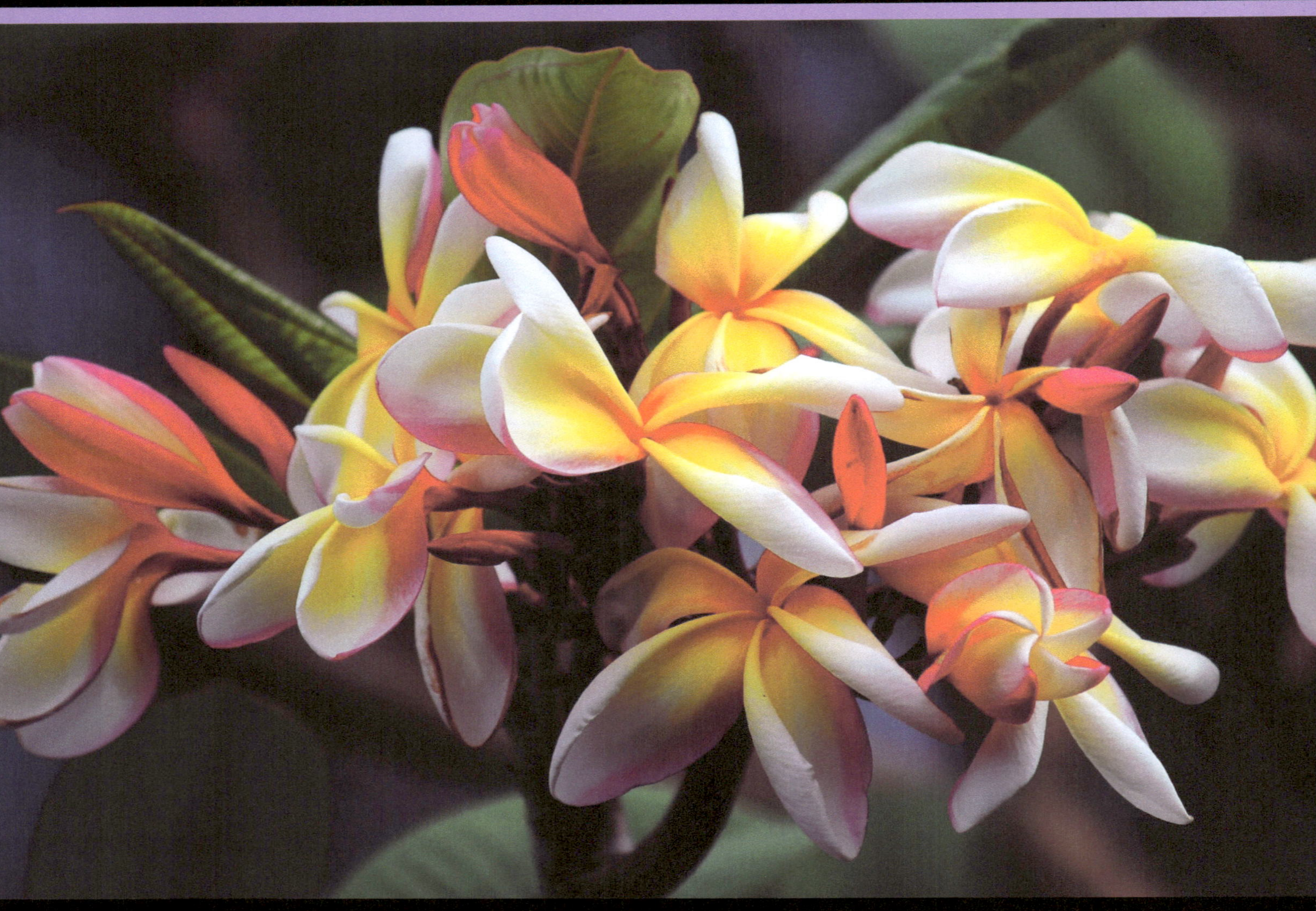

I laugh and I laugh. For the joy you give lifts me up out of misery. Do you remember how we met or the moment we shared love's first kiss? Or how I told you how much you liked it and the softness of your lips. We laughed and we laughed until we almost cried. That was the day that love healed my pride. And since that day, I have been free. I no longer pretend I am someone I don't need to be; because you love me. You love me...

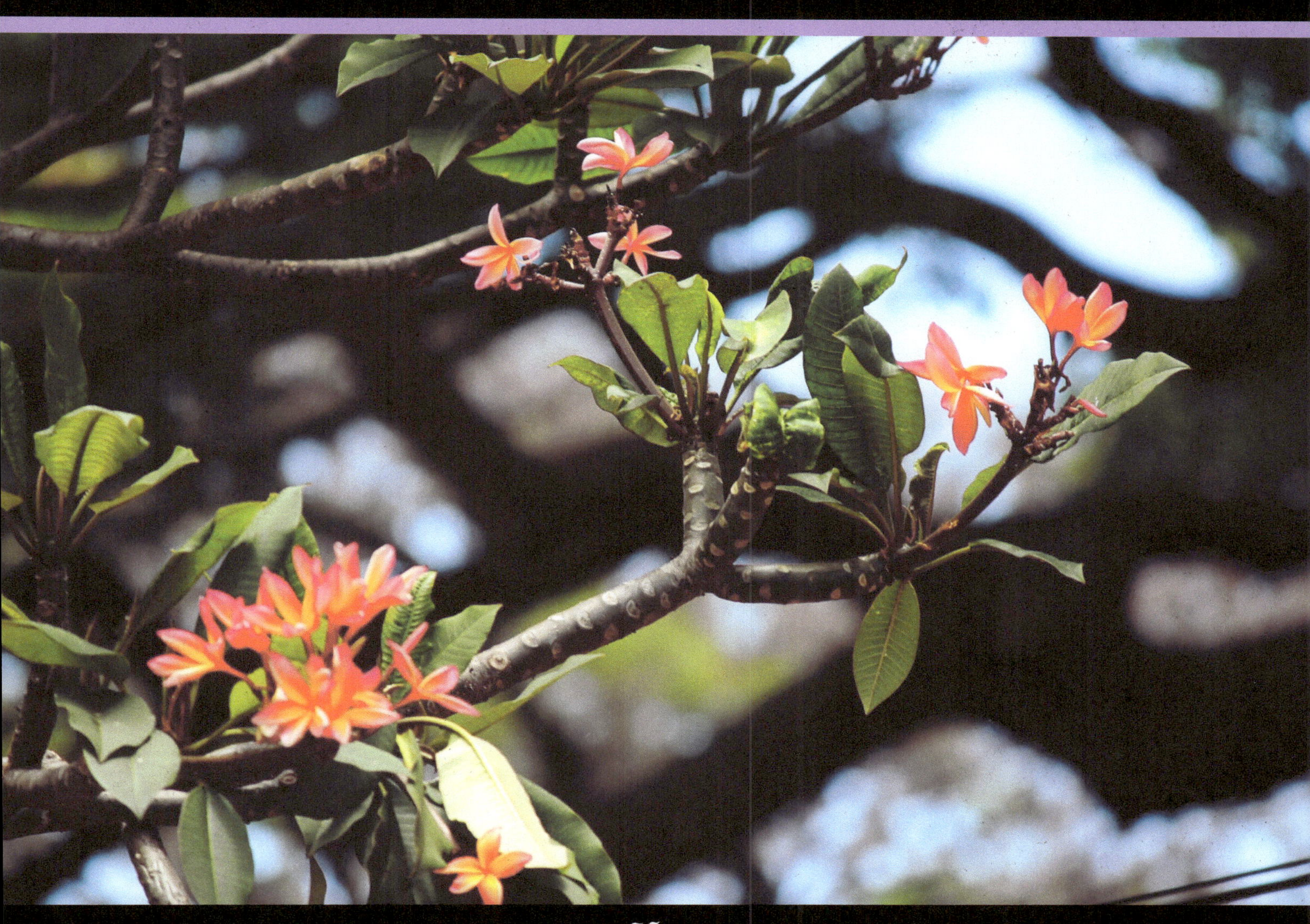

Come away with me... Let me take you to where dreams begin and never end... A paradise beneath the trees among the azaleas in the field. There beside a river bend by a lovely French country inn, where love awaits in a romantic secret place. Where the river plays our song and we join in and sing along... Love... How great life is when I am with you... Life.. How great love is when my love is you...

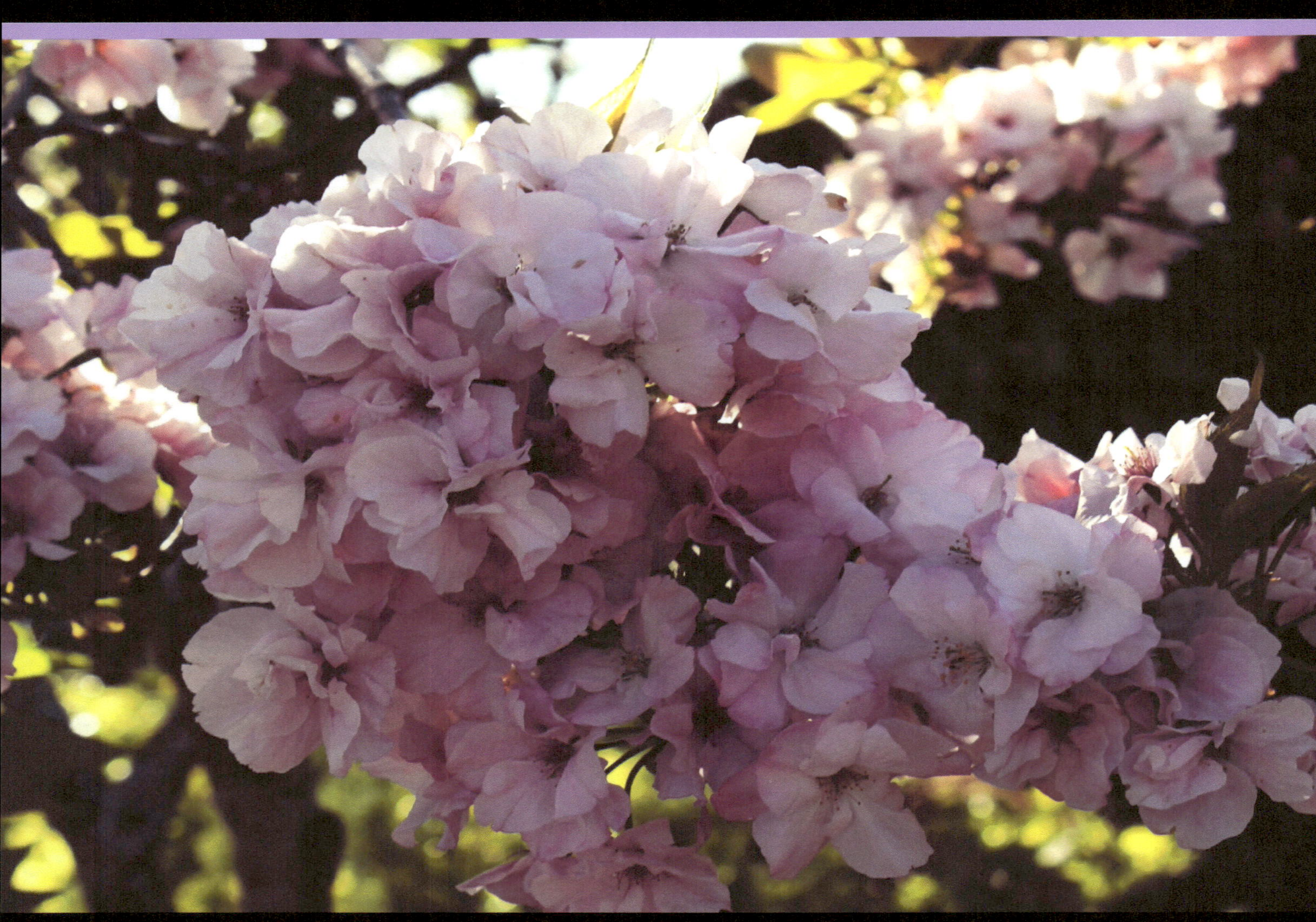

Love is the way you hold my hand when I'm a little ill. Love is the way you look at me when you ask me how I feel. Love is the way you lay my head against your rising breast. And when I close my eyes to sleep, love is how you're still with me when I wake and I see your face. Love is seeing you smile when I'm well again... Thank you for being my love... Thank you for being my friend...

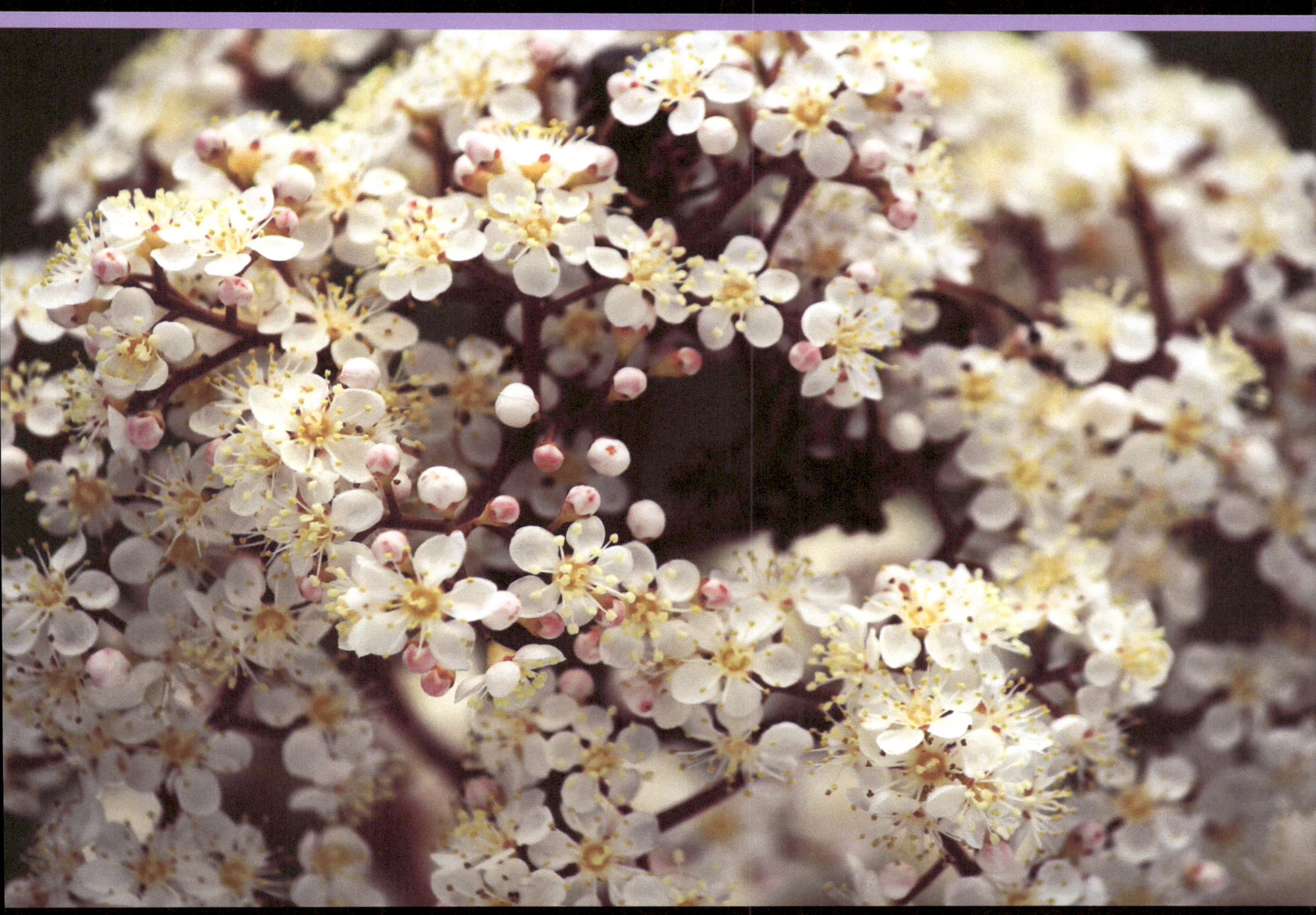

You have shown me love, and when I think of you, everything anguishing just disappears. Thoughts of you remind me of how good life can be. I am surrounded by your effervescence of hope; floating on a cloud of peace. You have entered my world and made what was wrong turn right before my eyes. You have brought me faith and faith have saved my life.

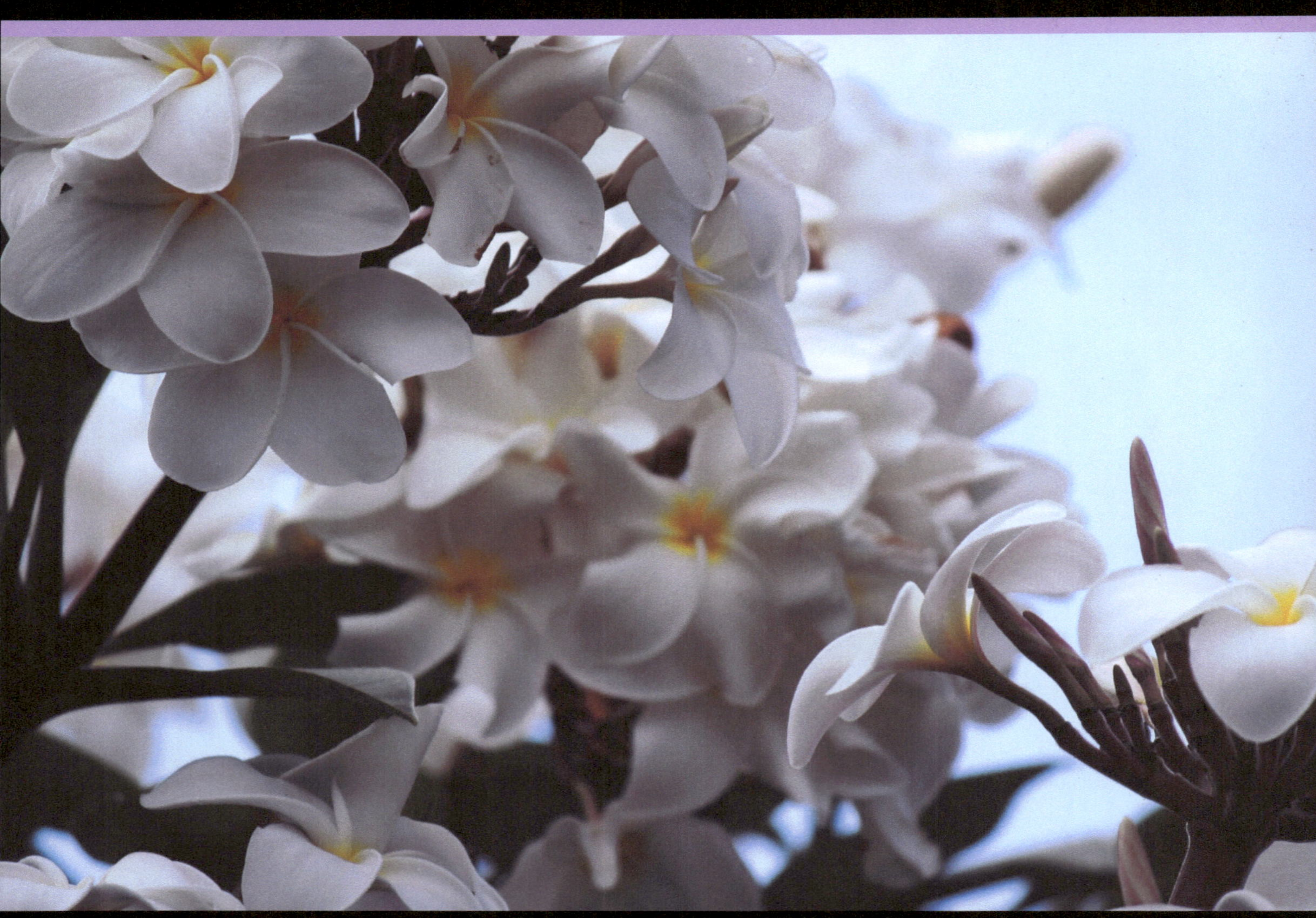

Where are you now, my lover, my friend? I search the memories of my dreams so our love will never end. Where are you my true love; I reach for you with my mind and we are not far away. How I miss you dearly; no one could ever you replace. Think of me tenderly as I do you. And remember me fondly as my arms remember embracing you. Soon, my darling, we shall be together again. I will gladly defy time to be your lover again...

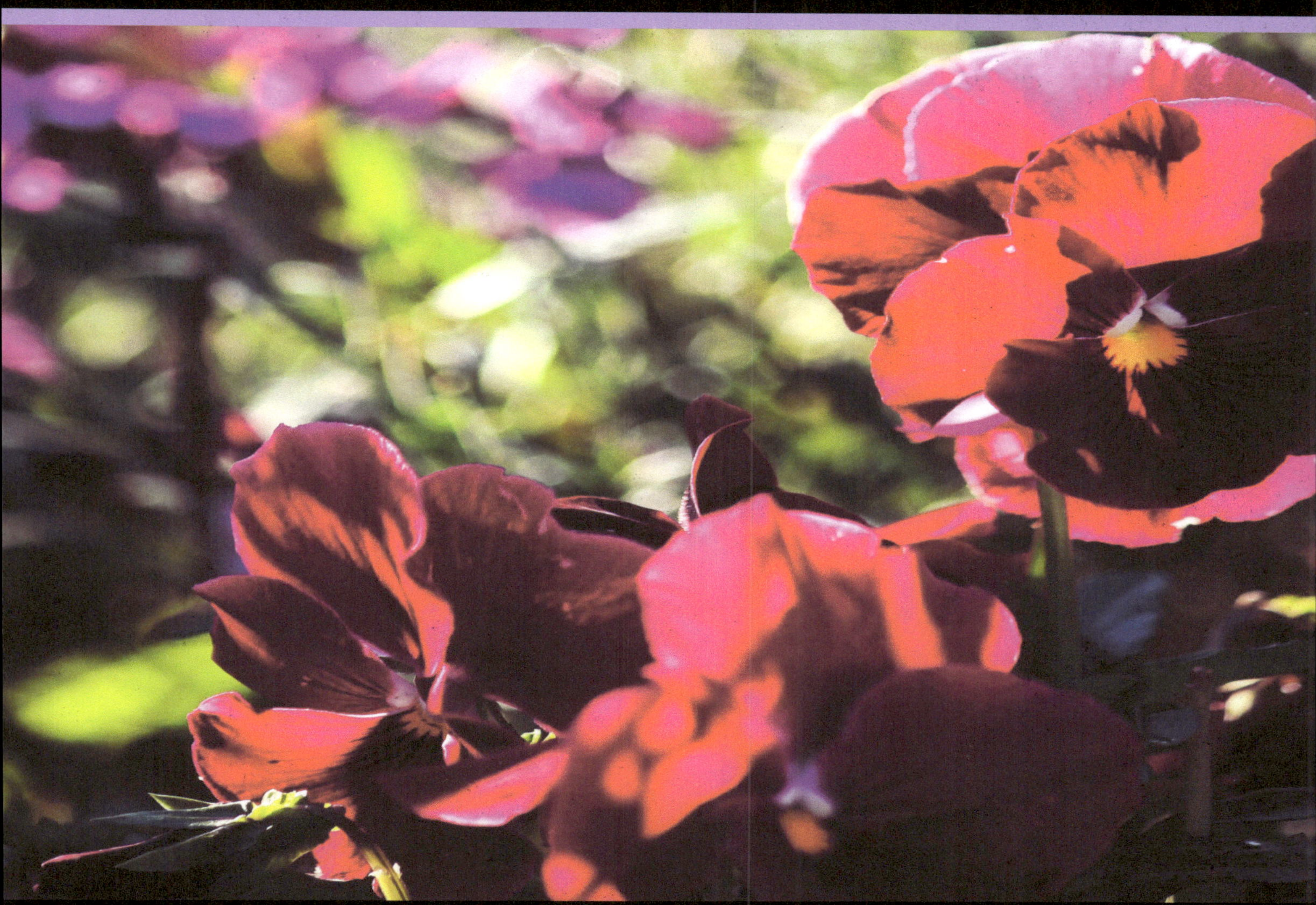

Promise me the starry nights when we gaze up at the moon. Promise me the sandy shores where the sun glistens at noon. Promise me the herbal scents of the fields we roam at dawn. Promise me the rich verdure of a tender Sunday morn. Promise me the soft caress from the gentleness of your arms... Promise me a tender kiss that will last my whole life long...

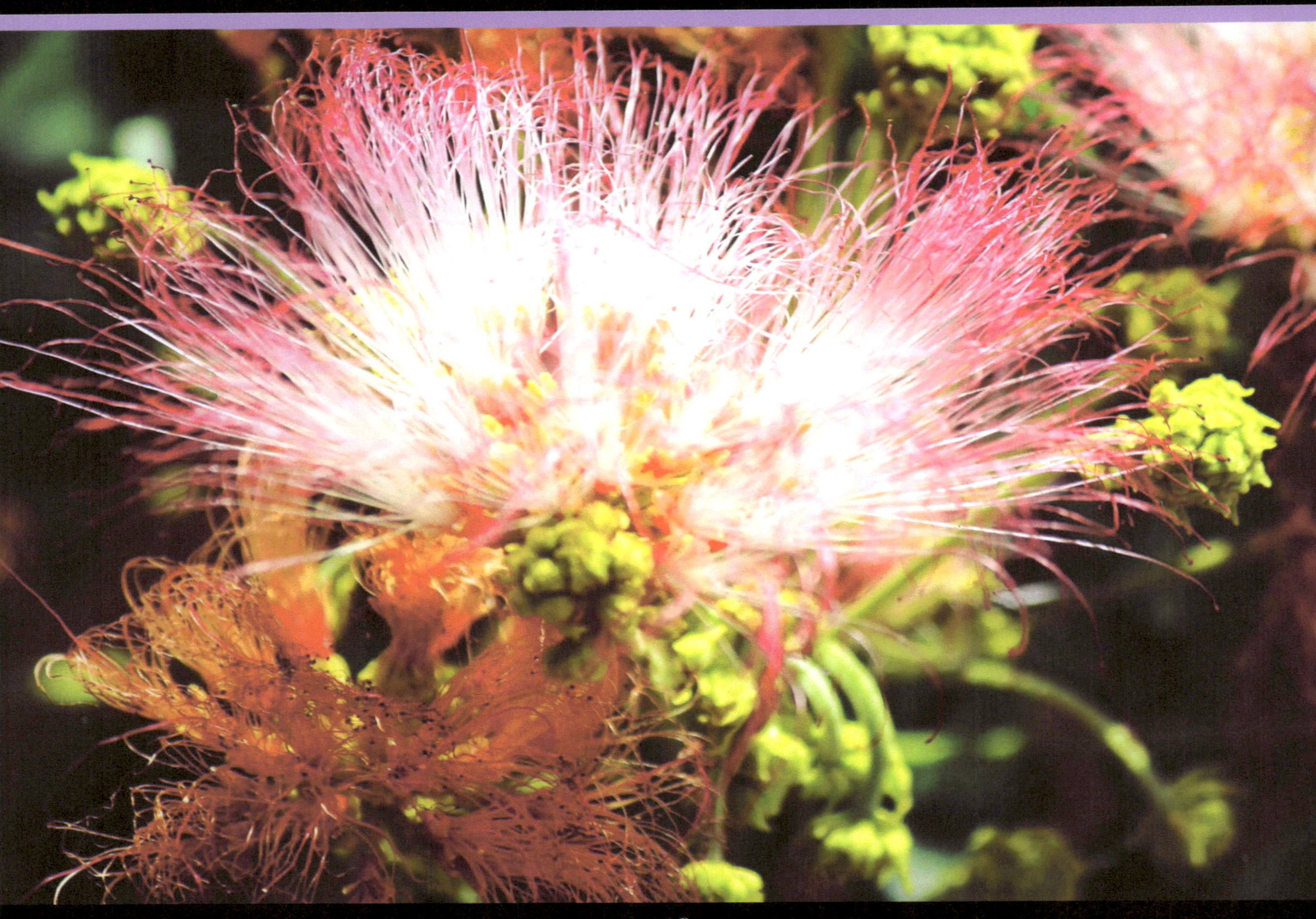

Mon amour, did you know that I can't wait for you to walk through my door? Did you know that I bathe with you lying in my arms? Did you know that you give me pleasure in my mind? Did you know that you command my desires? Can you guess what I have on my mind? Hurry... I can't wait; we're racing against time.

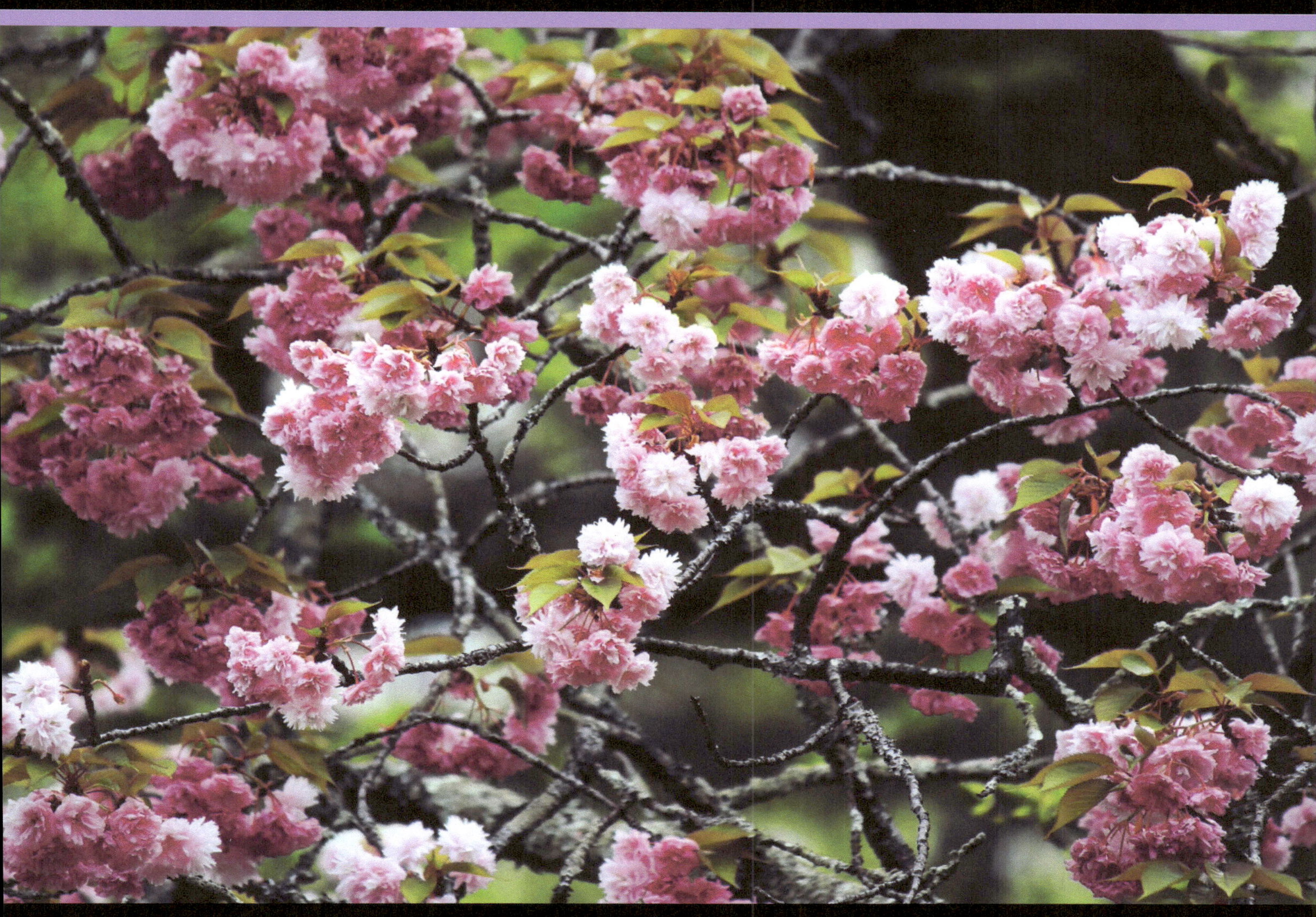

I know you... for you have revealed yourself to me. I have seen a glimpse behind the walls of your unknown. The mystery of your brokenness, the fears of your heart. Trust me with your tenderness and confide in me with your kiss, and you shall know me intimately and we shall heal together in passionate bliss...

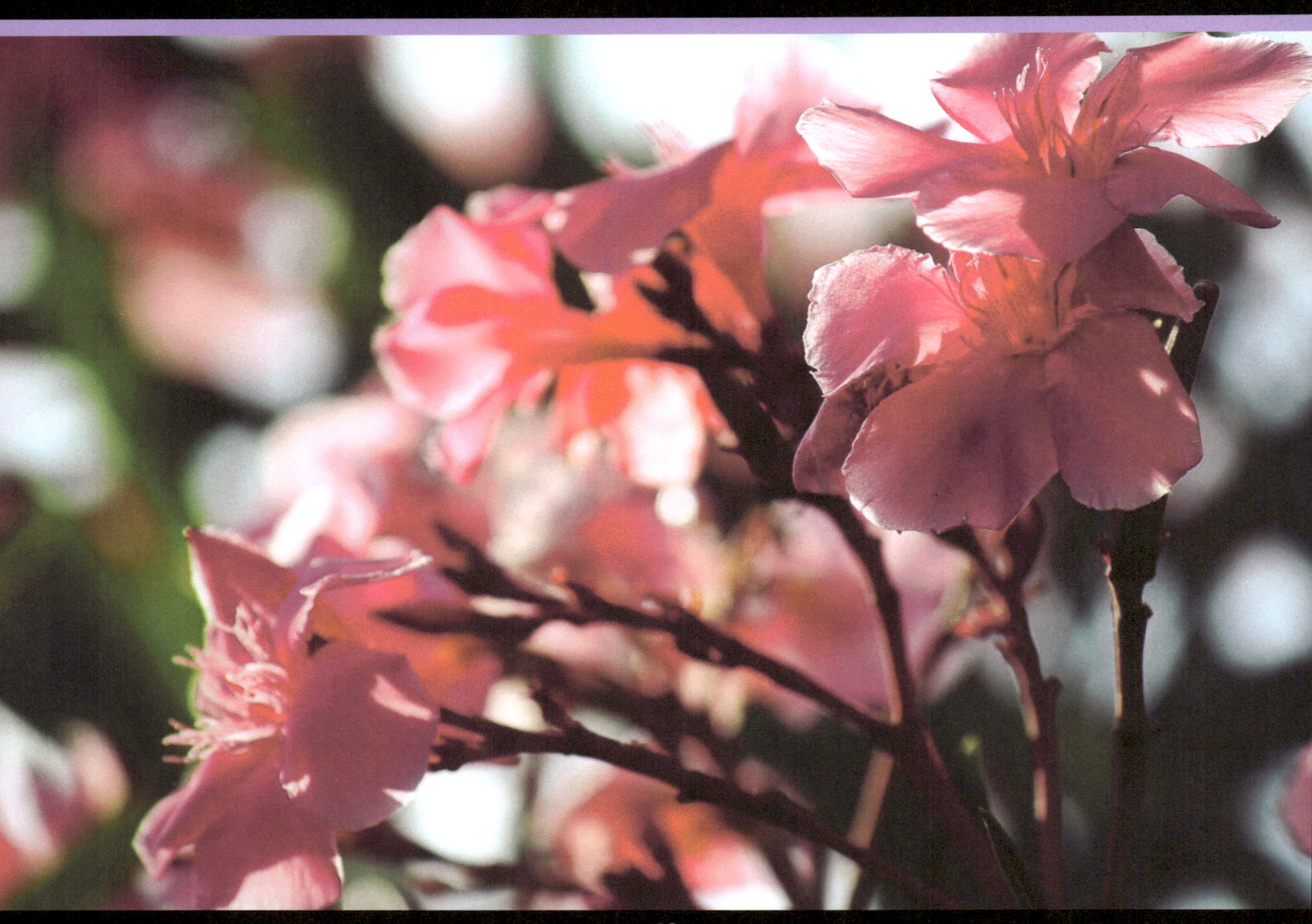

If you need me, I will be there for you. If you love me, I will give my world to you. If you want me, I'll fill your hungering void. Whatever you need, whatever you want, whatever you desire and all you are aching for, I am the answer to your prayer. For I am love, and I am everything you need and encompass all you dream.

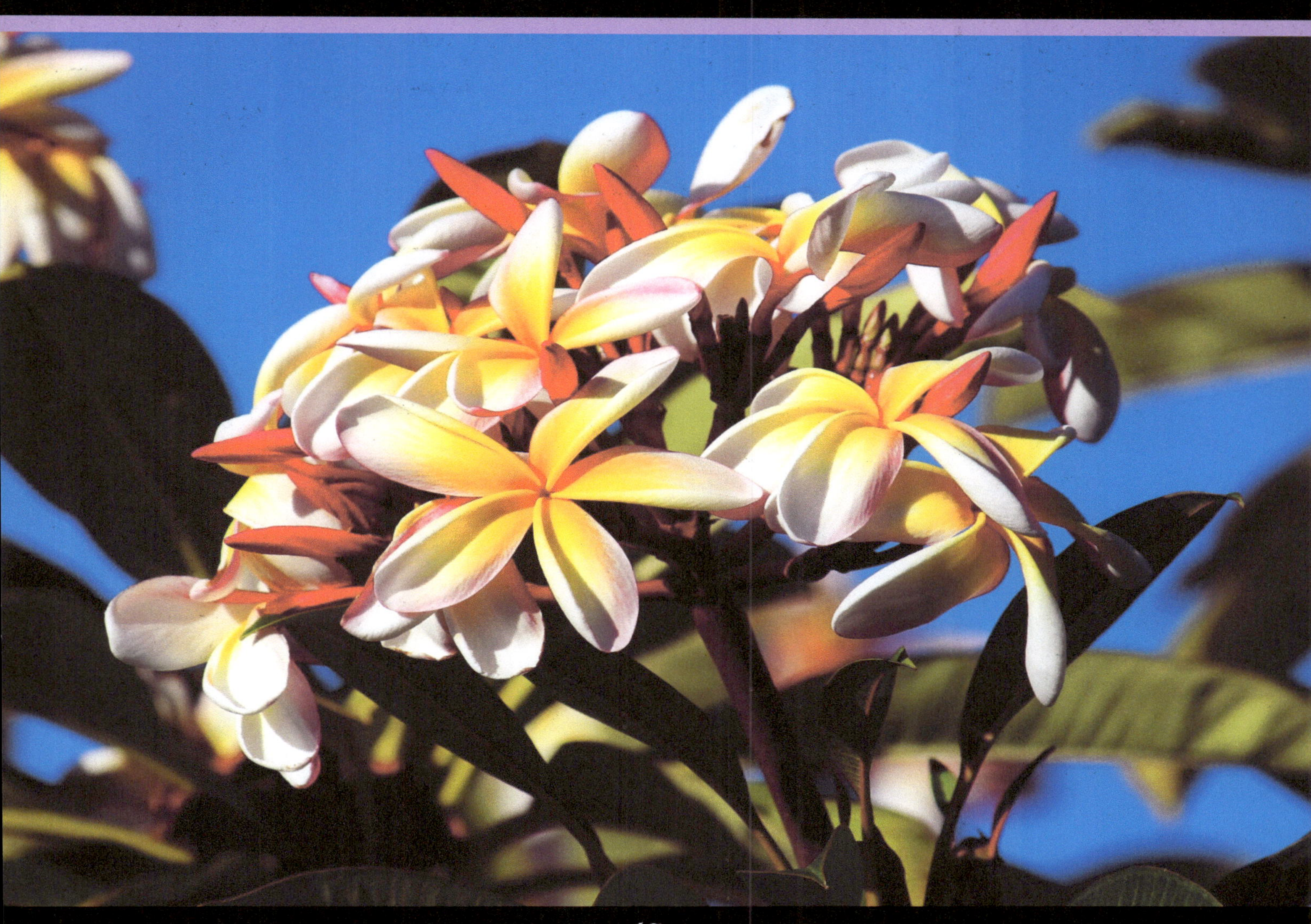

I will comfort you in the rain. I will shield you from the pain, and I will risk my heart again and again... I will... I will hold you when you cry, and wipe the tears from your eyes... I will stand right by you side... I will... And when all is said and done, and the darkest days are gone, I will lead you into the sun... I will...

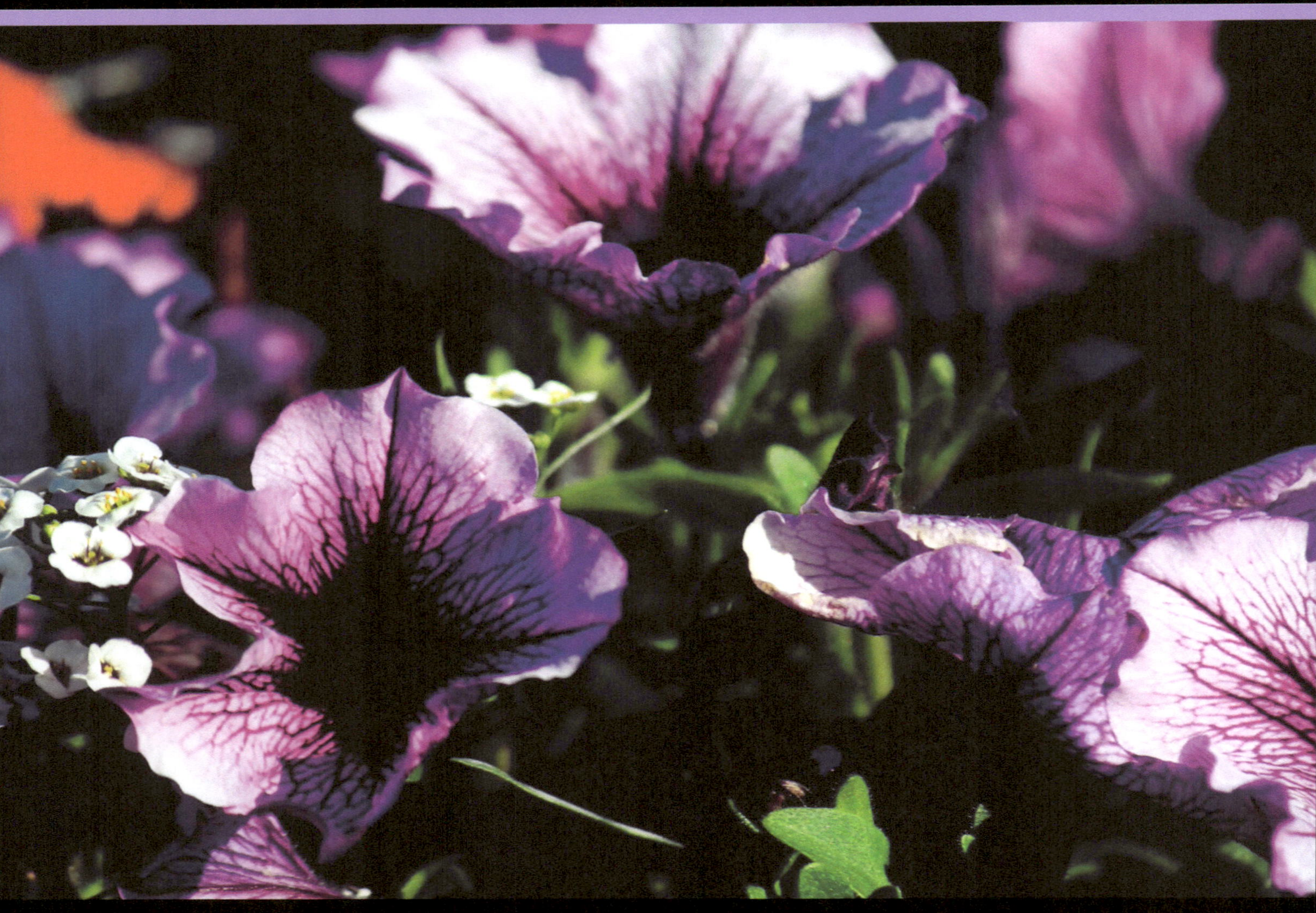

Put your hand in mine as we walk along the sea... And the wind kisses your hair as I hold you close to me. Feel the sand beneath your feet as the breeze caresses your cheeks, and the worry of what will be fly away. We are here and we are now. The pain of yesterday is gone...the memories both bitter and sweet. Today, we are free...

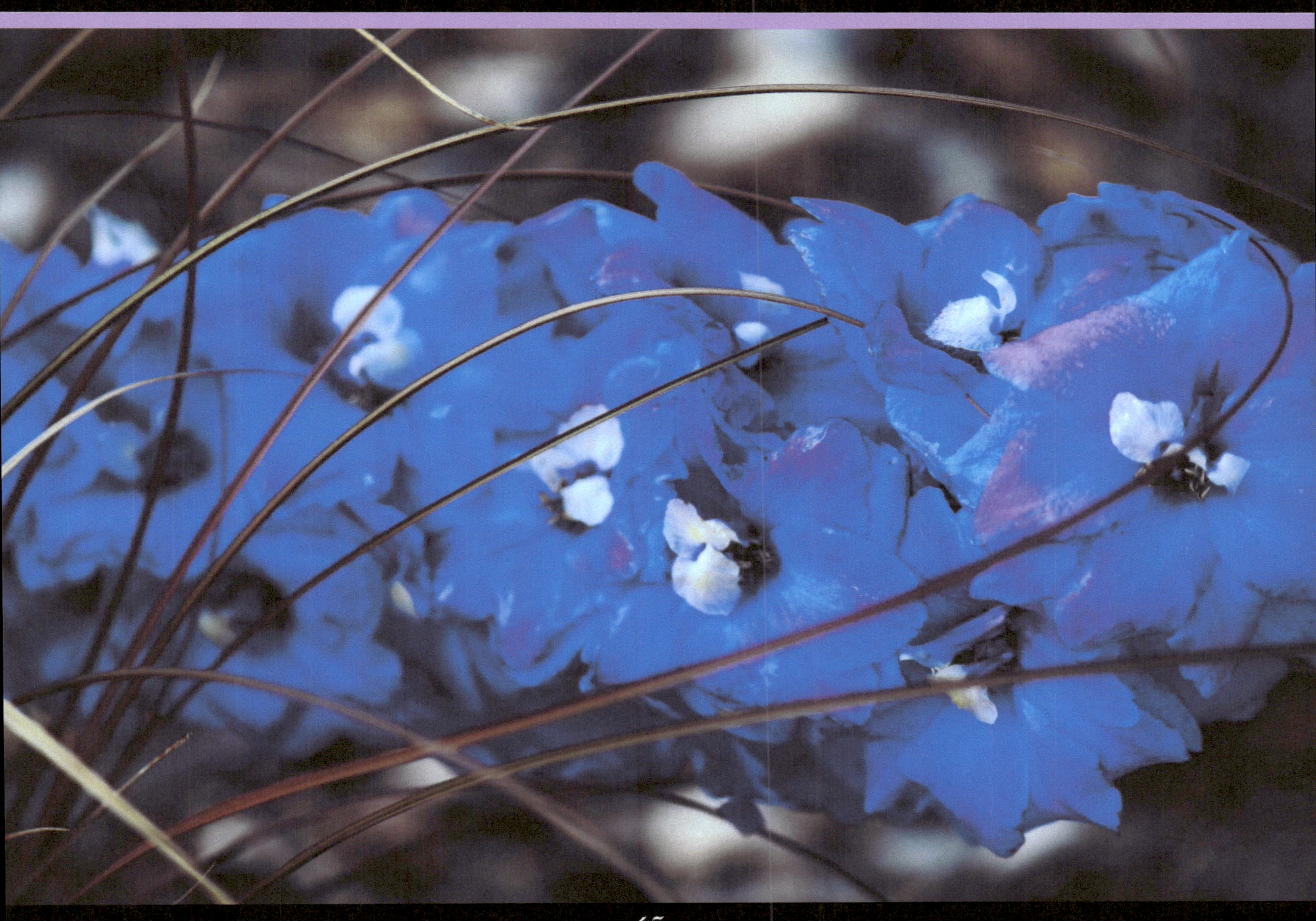

Sweet love... I taste your dew drops against my lips... Young love, young hope...so full of laugher and faith. Let us live long, let us love pure, and let us give without regret... And when our dying days are near, let us not weep; let us not fear, for our time together was well spent on love's rich moments of peace.

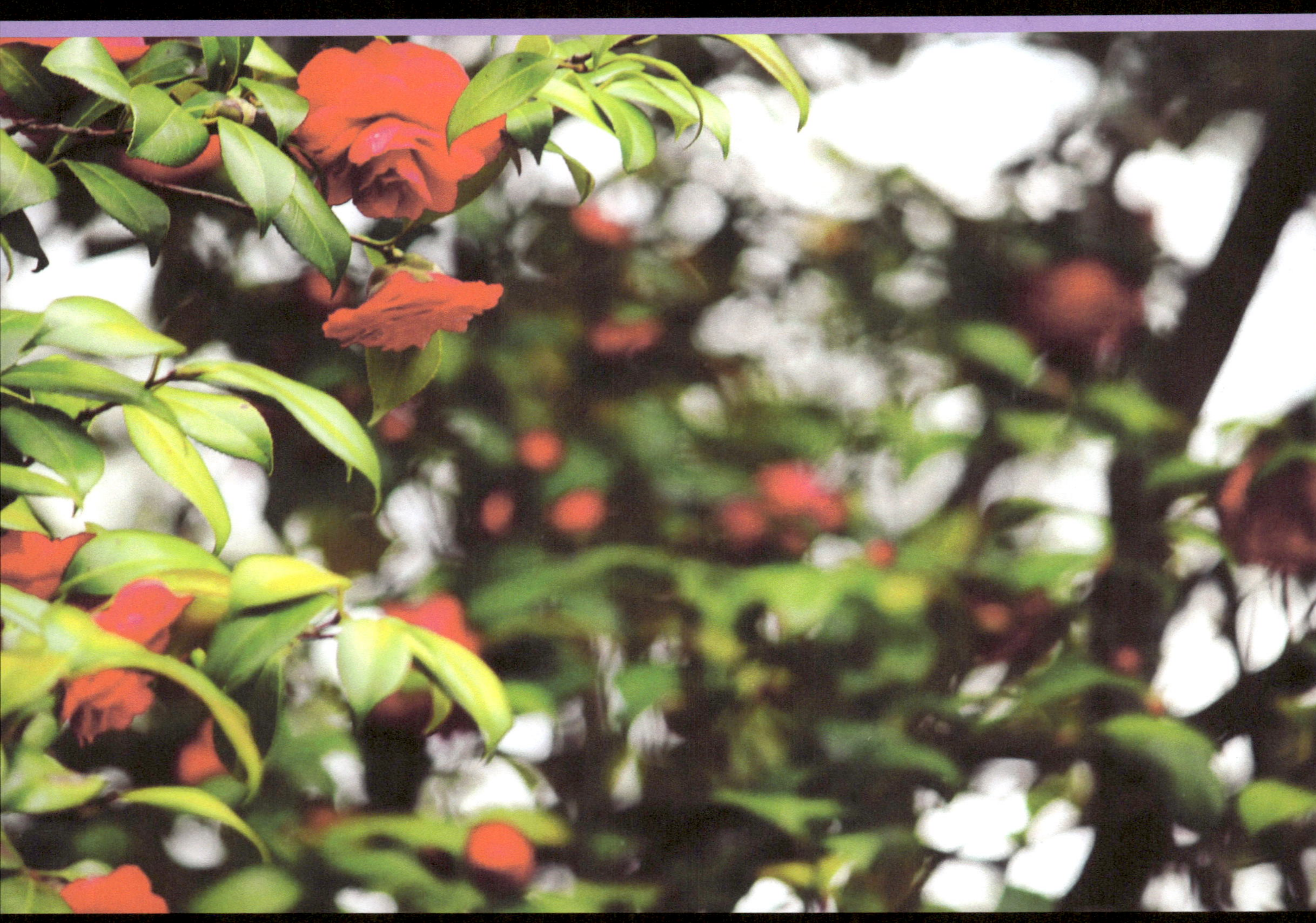

Oh, my Beloved, you are ripe for the tasting. Your sugary kisses are so sweet. The time has come for love making; reaping our orchard of ecstasy. Generosity is your harvest and my arms are already full. We are pressing our desires together, making wine out of love. Drink of me and be happy... Sip and be fulfilled... For true love is our bounty, and I am drunk on your nectar of love...

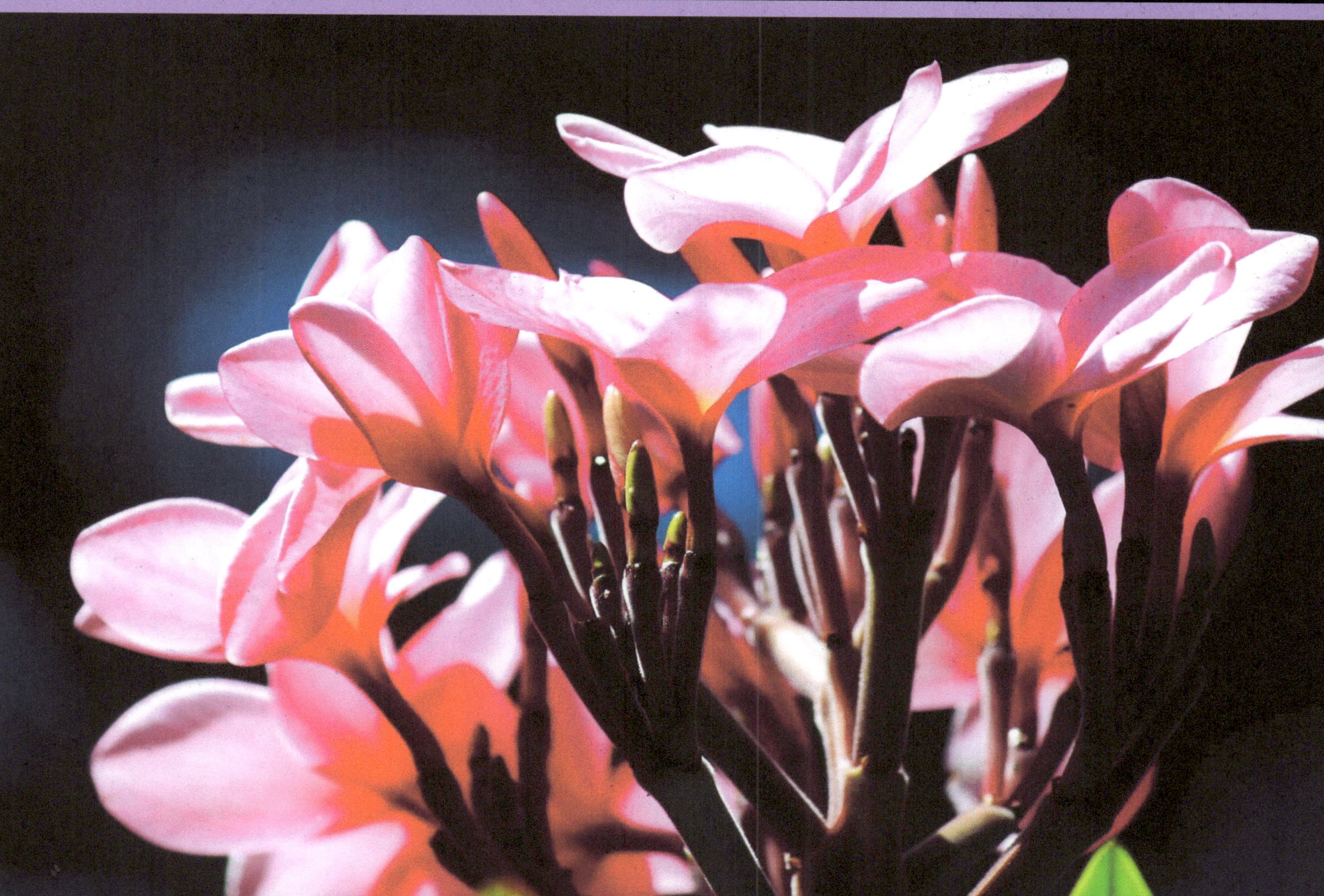

I must confess... My favorite painting has etchings of your face. I've been in love with you since the moment you smiled my way. If I shared my secret, how my heart whispers of your name and I finally reach for you, would you do the same? Tell me now if you feel the way I do. Do you love me as I love you? Then our secret will become our most treasured gift, and my confession will bear the truth with a loving passionate kiss...

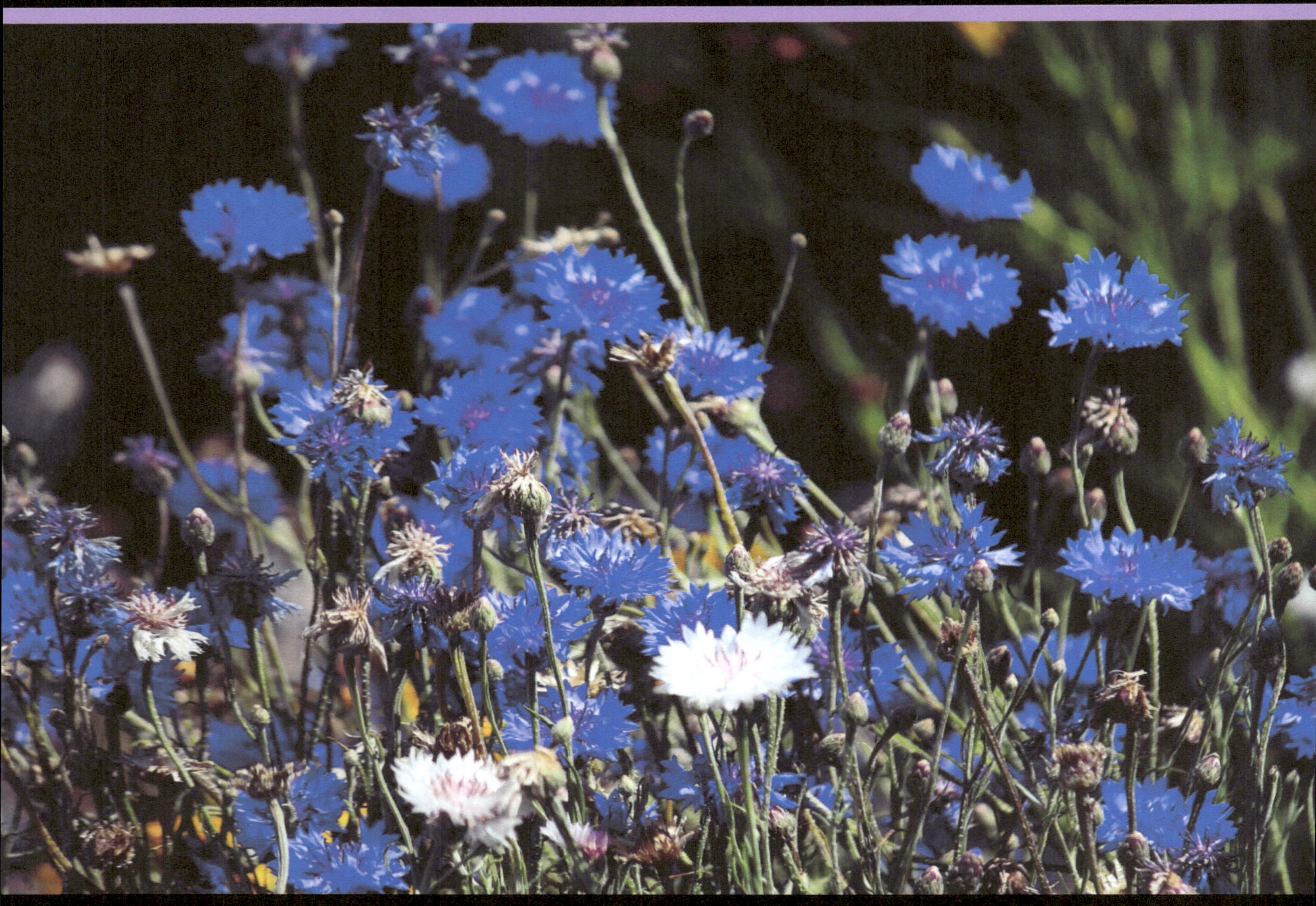

Speak to me all that your heart desires. Confide in me all that you dare to divulge. I am among your greatest supporters. I will cheer you on when you need to believe. My darling, you are my inspiration. Your beauty is the like heaven's spring. The earth has so much need of you, but God is surely missing her most beautiful being.

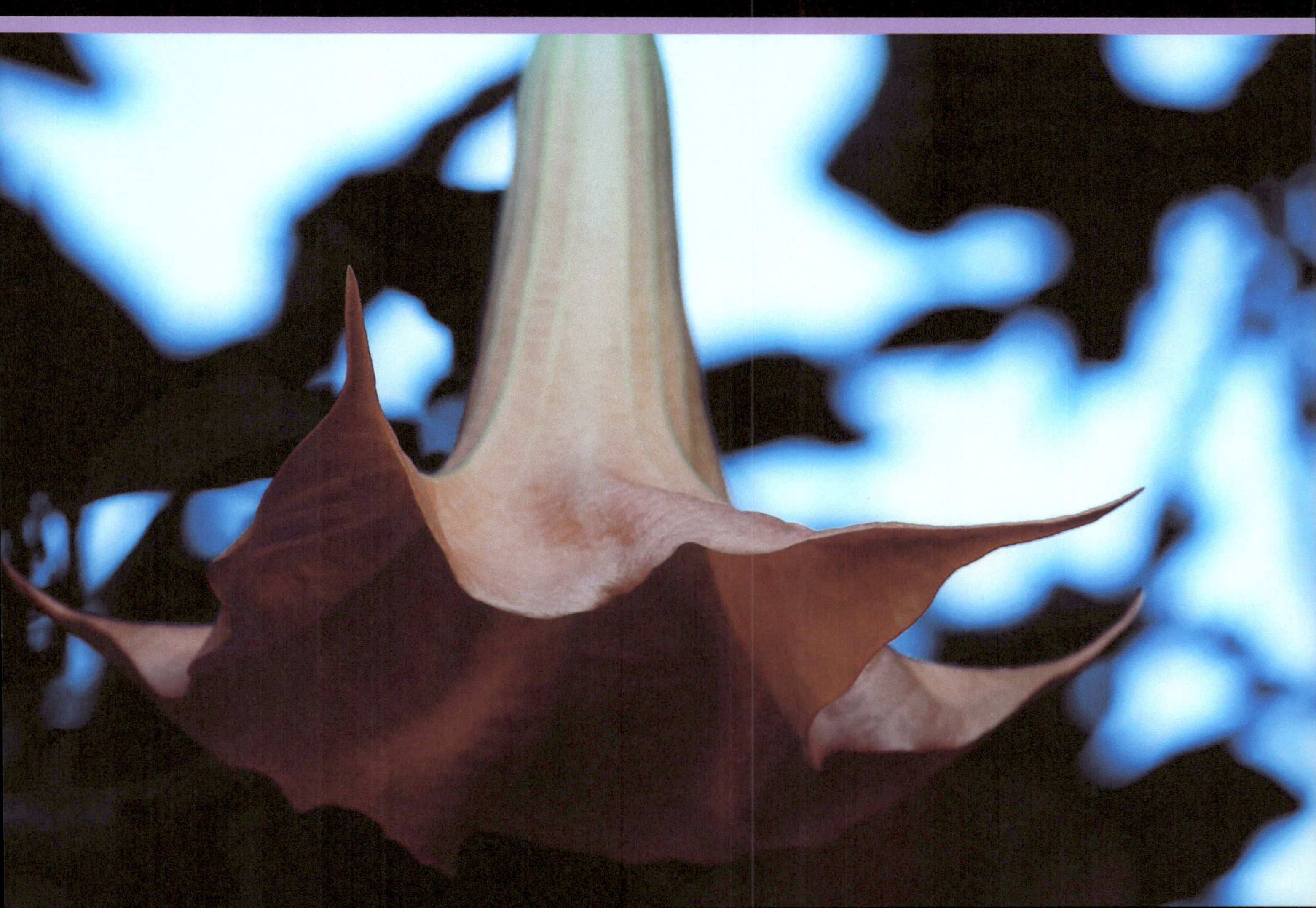

I love you with no walls, no masks, and no lies. See who I am. There is nothing that I hide. I am true... I am sure... My heart is open and pure. Look in my eyes... I do not lie. No... You have all of me and I give all that I am. Believe me when I say, no other will have my heart. I am in love with you...

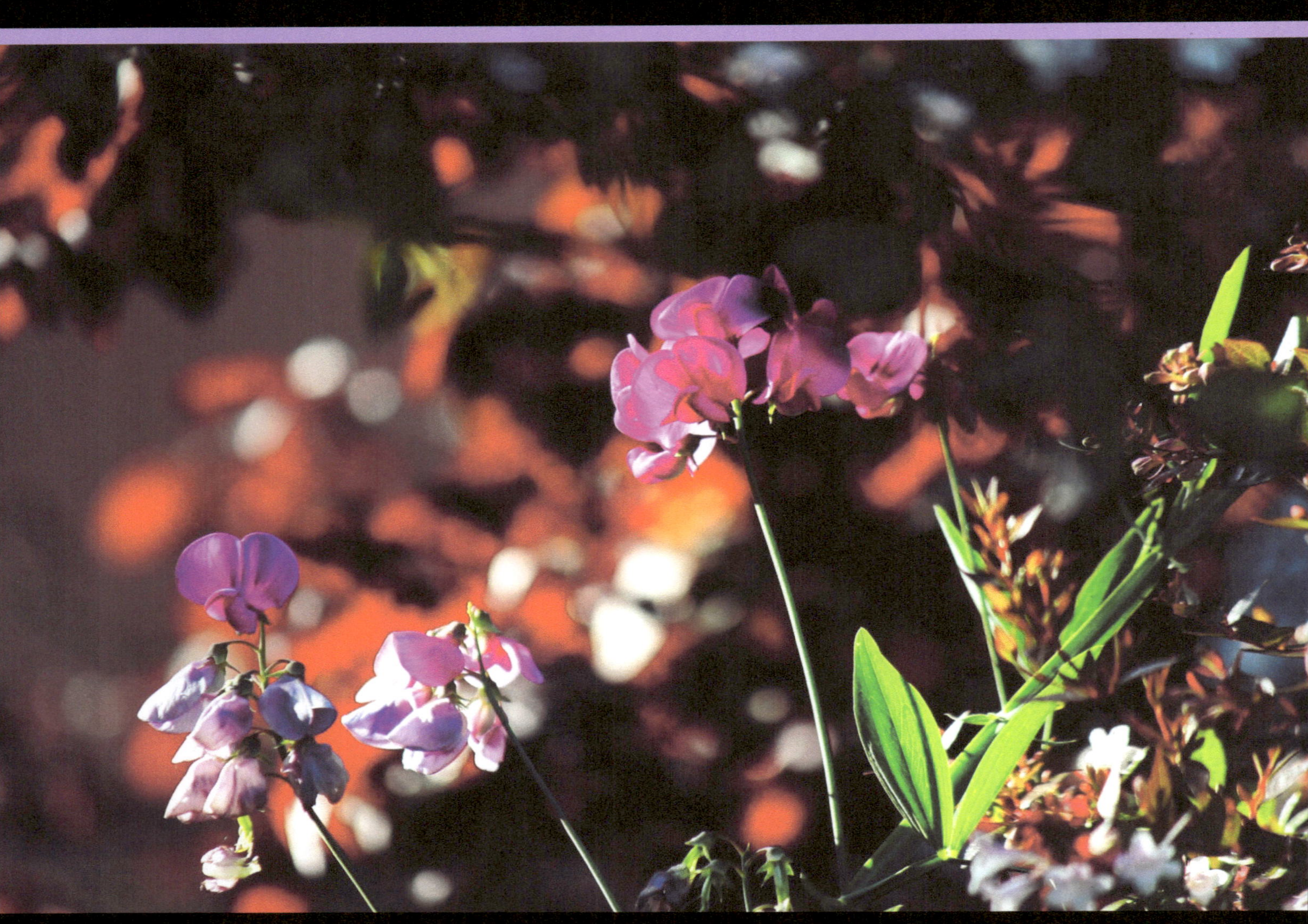

We will laugh in the rain as we run hand in hand, just you and I. We will dance cheek to cheek and kiss beneath the sheets, and toast our love with wine. We will wallow in our dreams and do all or nothing. And we will live among the stars from dusk until the dawn. We will be lovers reborn, just you and I...

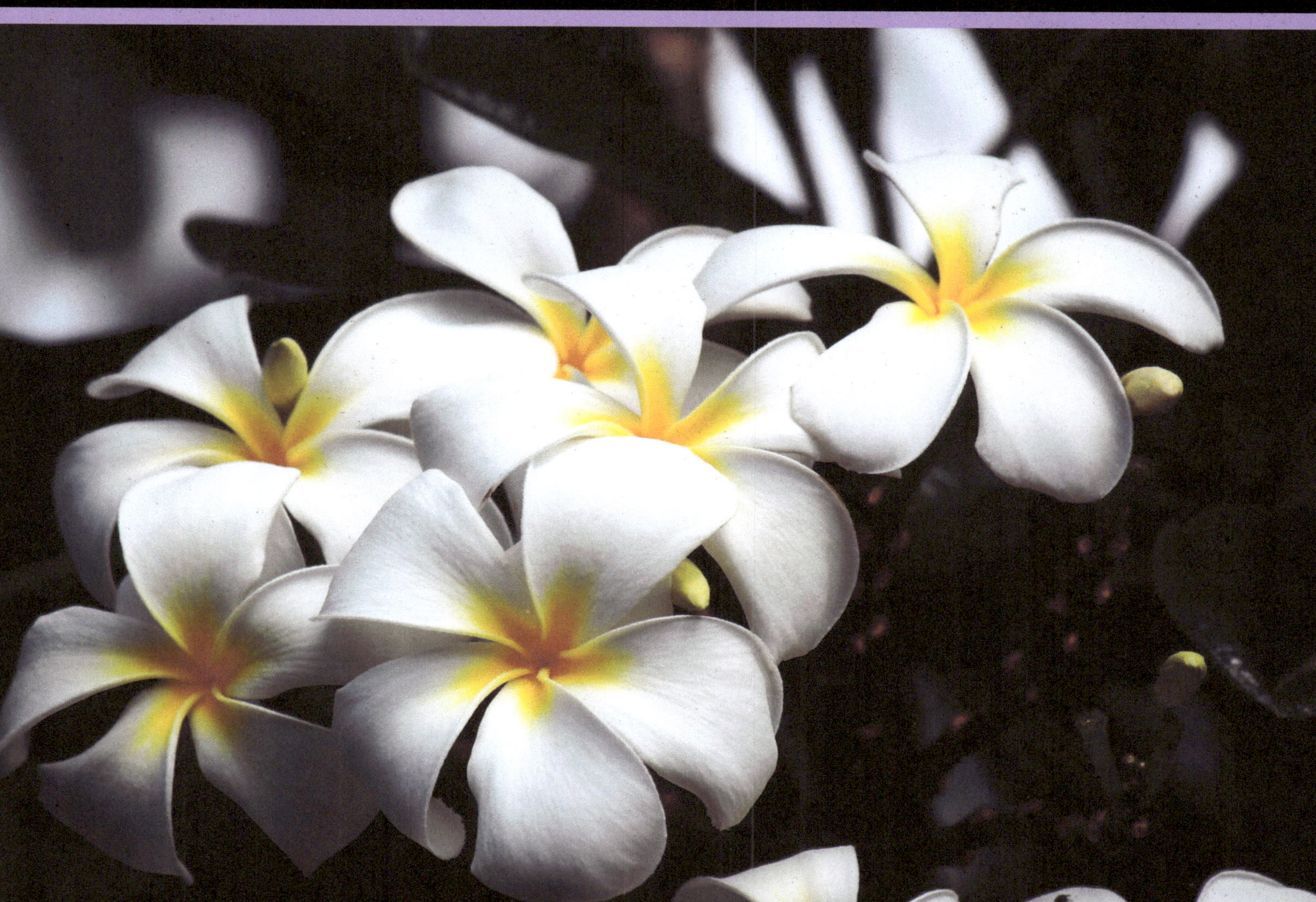

Let me lead you to paradise, my beautiful dove. Let me take you to a place where we can explore love. Oh, how I can't wait to revel in your smile, to kiss your mouth and explore all that encompasses you... I can imagine how good it will feel when we are face to face. My love will be as faithful as the rivers flows free. And I'll be pulled in your undertow. And we'll be as happy as lovers can be; our life, our love, our time, you and me...

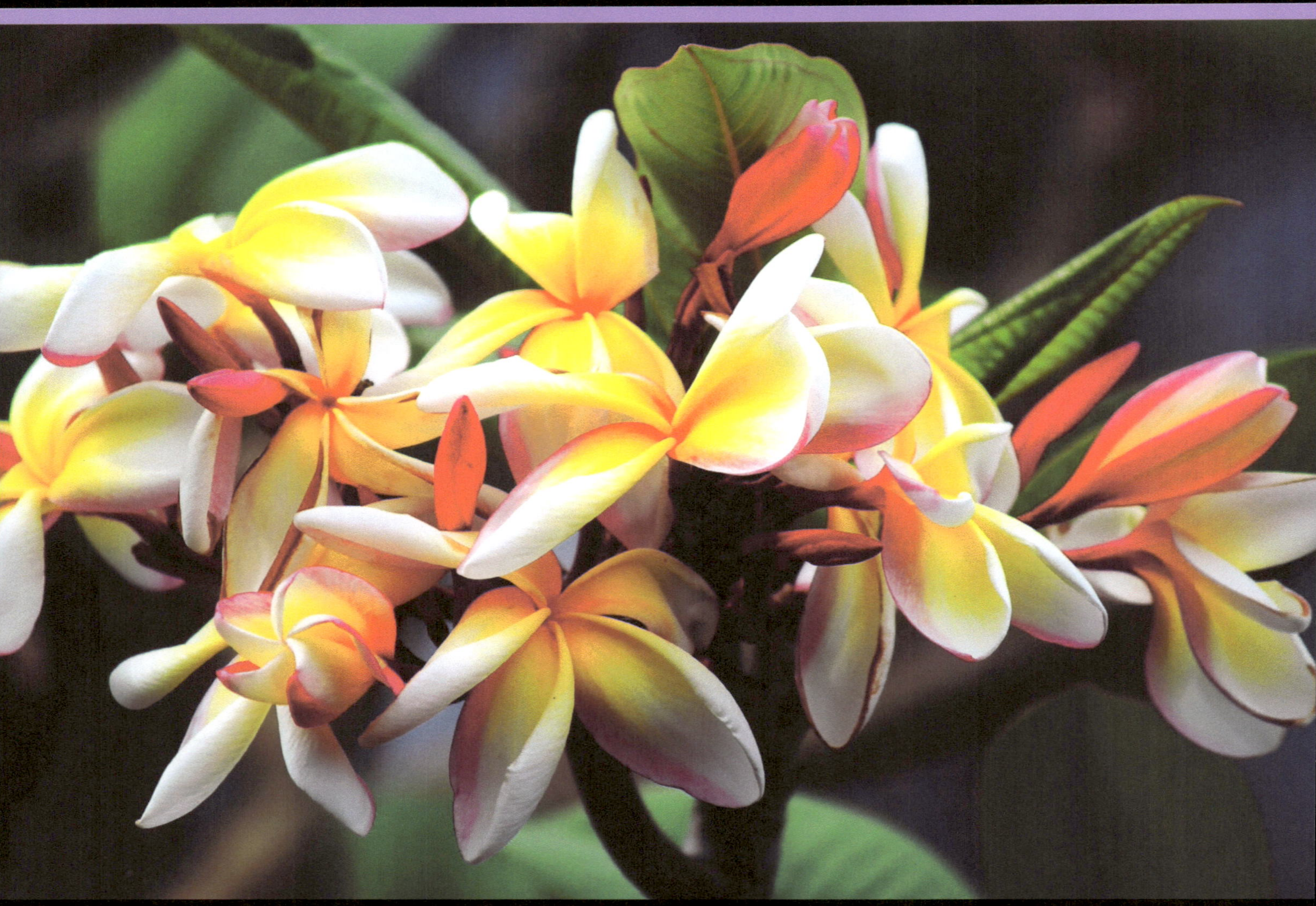

Your love is like a warm summer's day. I want to wrap my arms around you and carry you away. Away from the storm clouds and the worrying doubt, to encourage your dreams and lift you up. You touch my trembling heart and my life feels renewed. You save me from the frigid winter when I'm feeling blue...The way you love me, so gentle, so sweet, makes me feel wonderful to be alive. There's nothing I wouldn't give to keep your love.

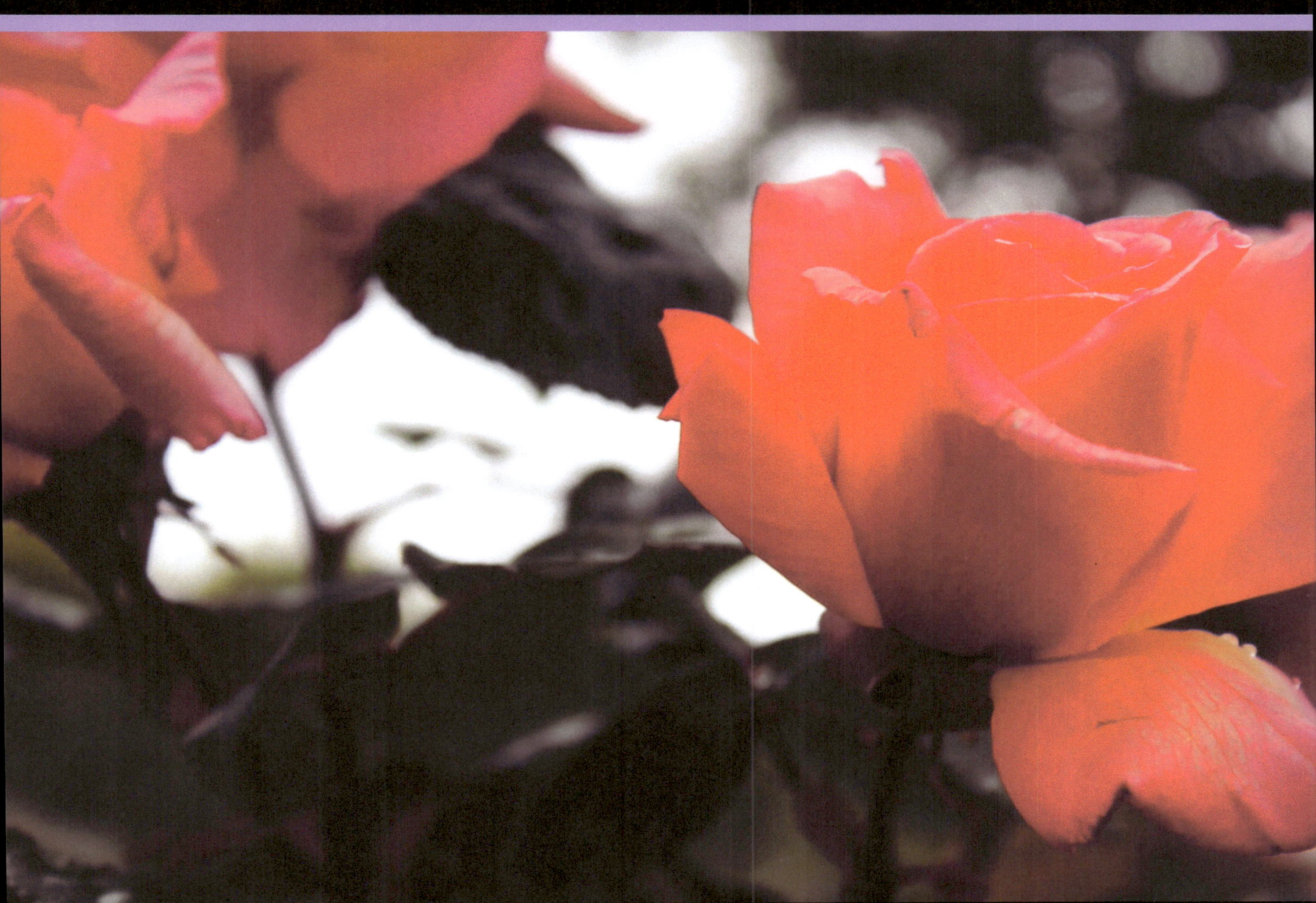

Your lips are like candy... Your skin like the feathers of a dove. Your hair is as soft as petals and your eyes are like sparkling jewels. Please indulge me; I have never seen someone so lovely, even your tears taste like wine. I am enthralled by your essence. I must proclaim you before the world... For you alone have my devotion and I am bedazzled by you and your love is mine...

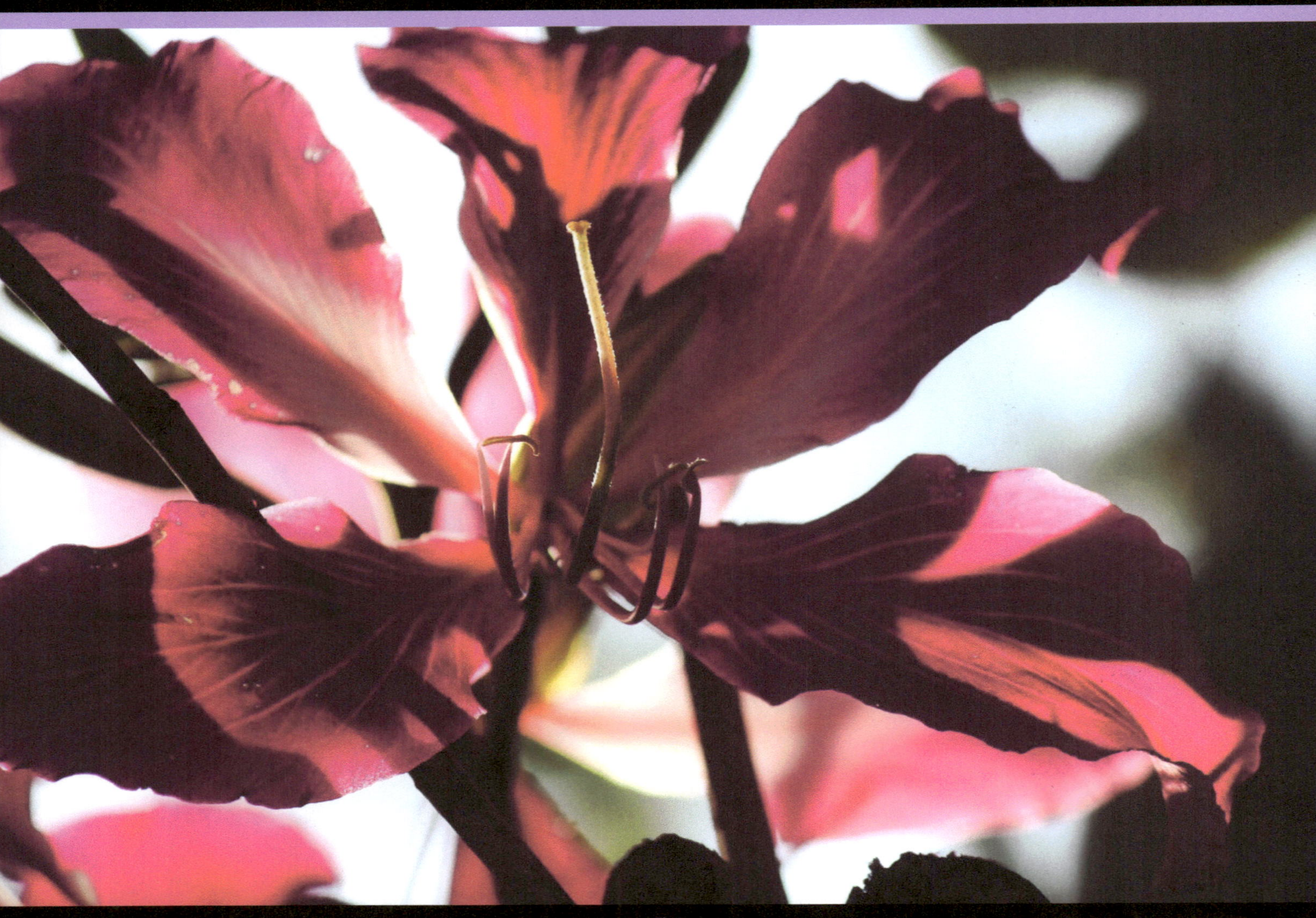

Your kisses are like honeysuckle dripping from your lips. My heart beats faster as I nuzzle your silky hair. And we sway to the music and dance like lovers on fire. And the worries that once enslaved our minds us disappears for while. And I release an urgent message as I whisper in your ear; for in this moment nothing but our love matters and the rest can wait until never begins...

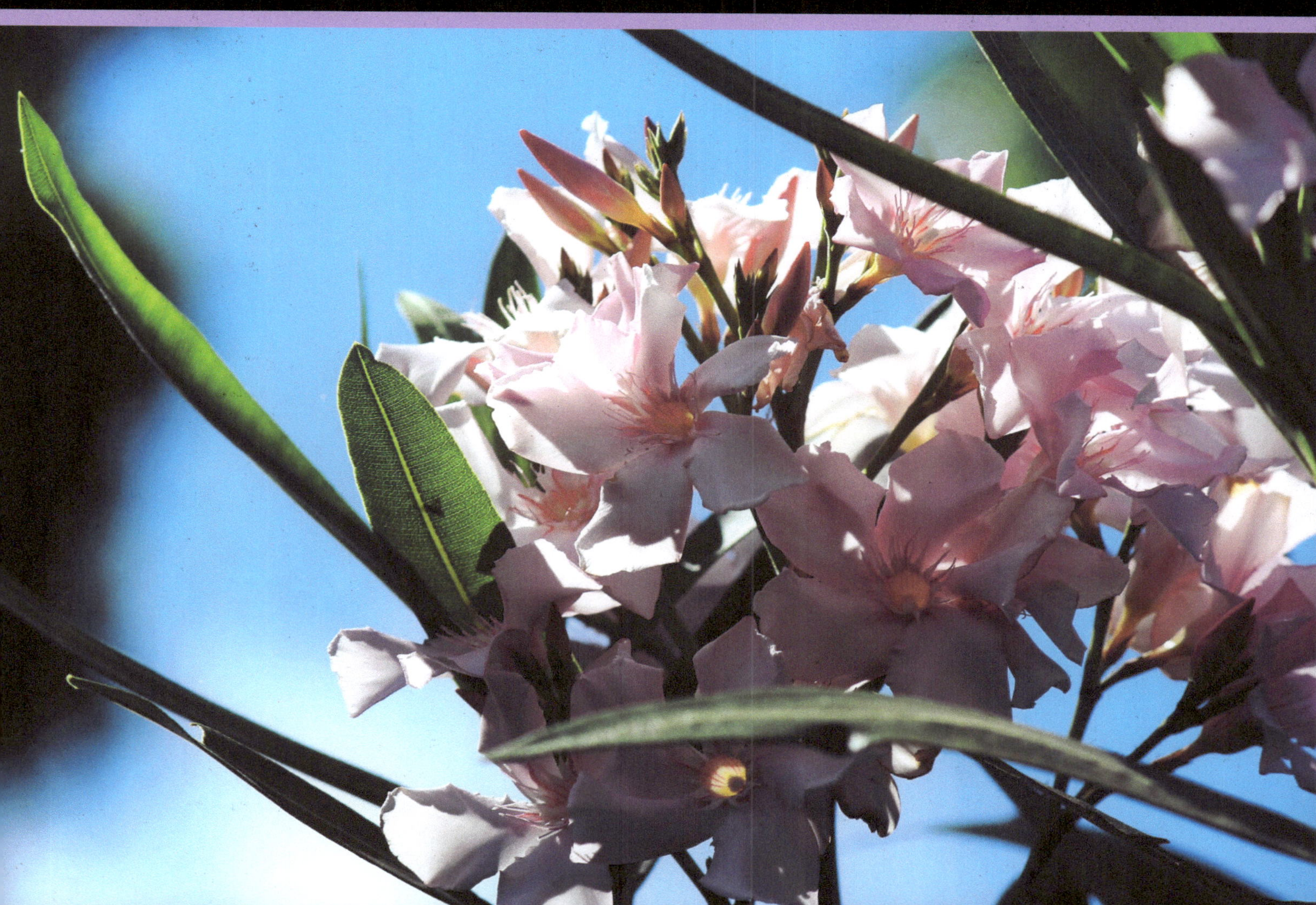

Lay down beside me, and hold me tight. I need you near me more than ever right now. Let your love rain down on me like rainbows glistening after the storm. Lay your head upon my shoulders, and let me hear your precious prayer... My love, my angel, your sweetness soothes my heart. My hurt heals with just the touch of your hands. And on your breadth of your wings, my soul floats on air...

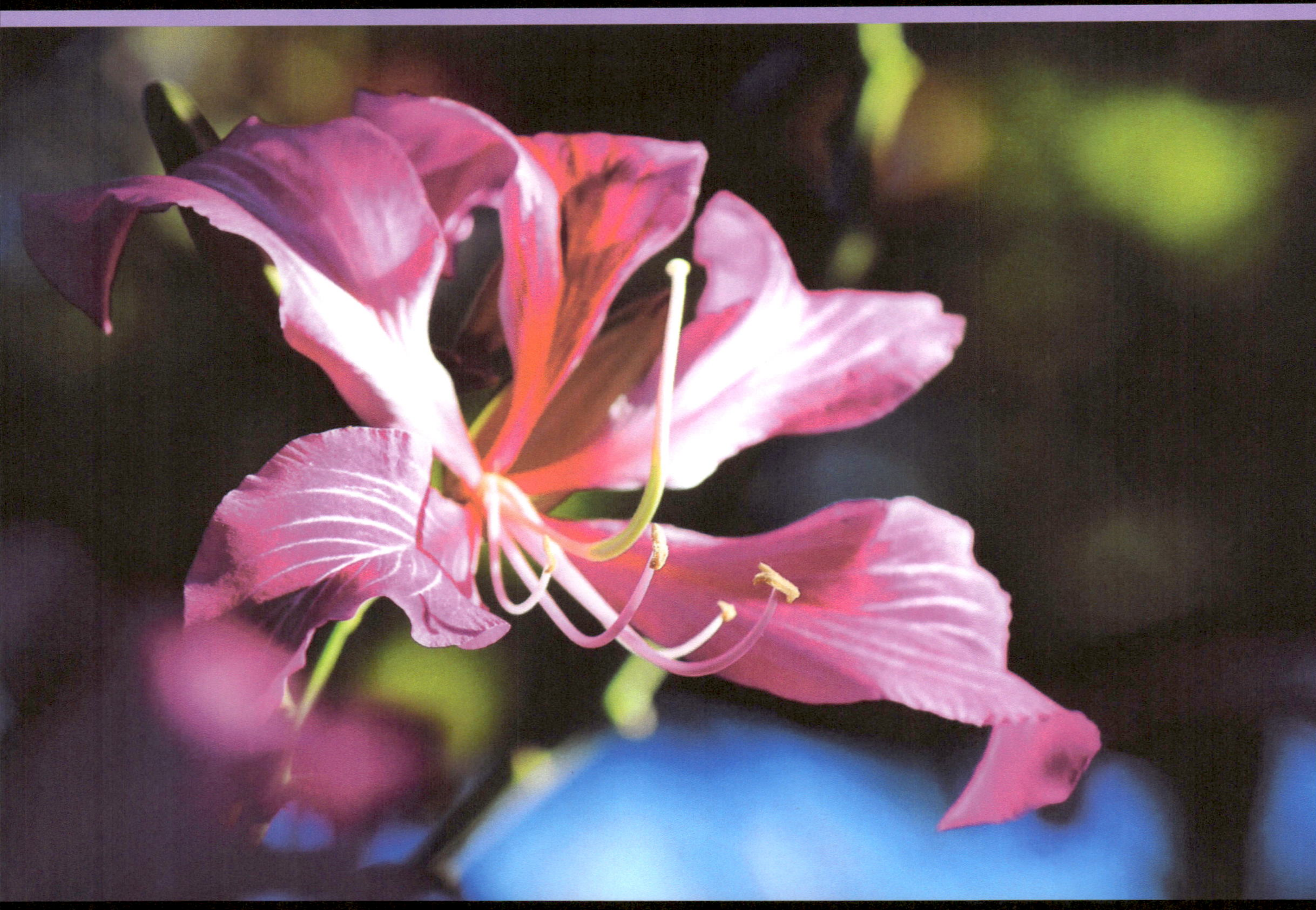

You are my love... My passion for you is deep. My words can only express a fraction of what I truly feel. For you bring to me more joy that any words could ever say. Thank you for being in my life; thank you for loving me. And thank you for teaching me how to give each and every day... You are my forever love and I am forever blessed because our love is here to stay...

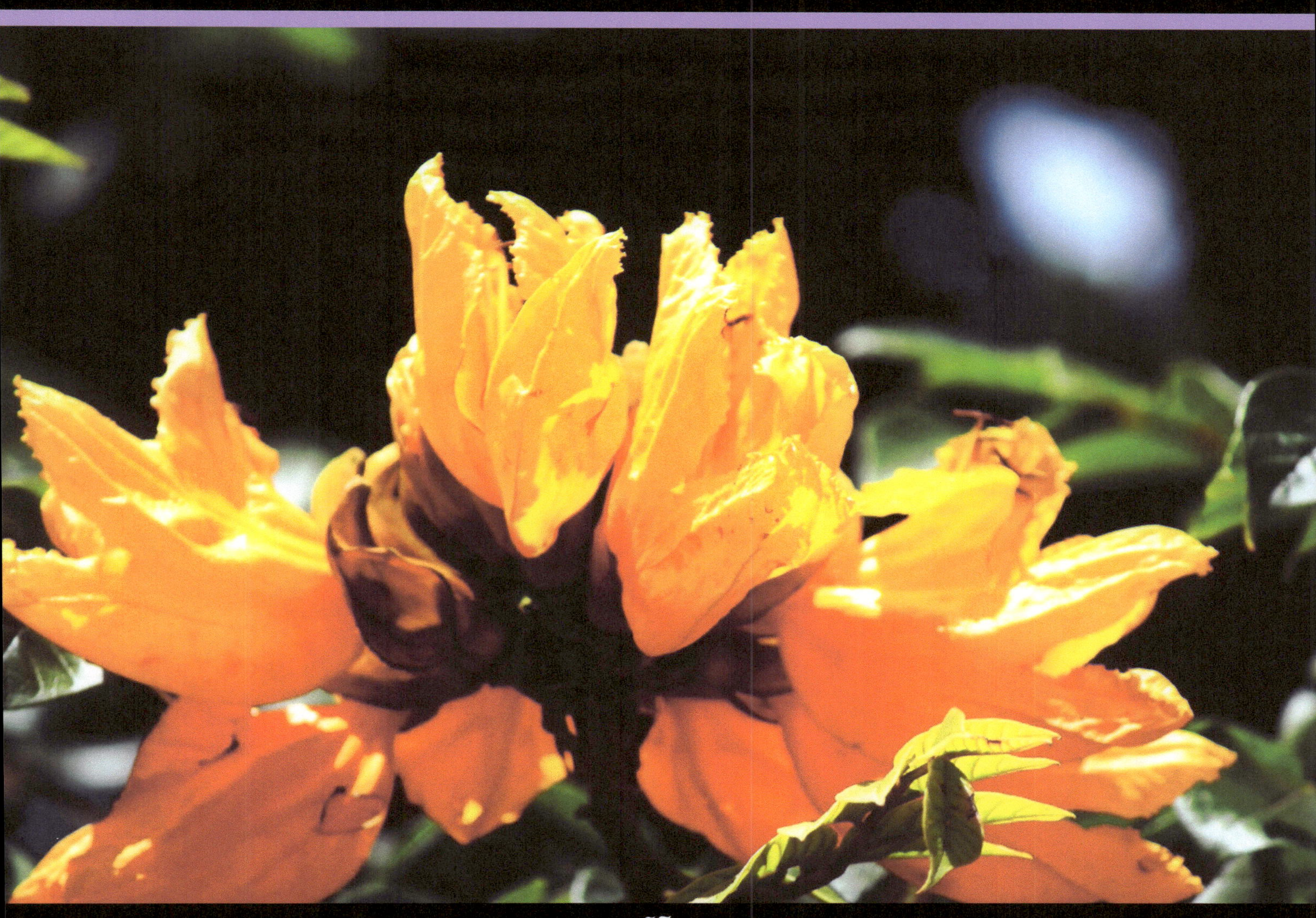

When I see your smiling face you brighten up my day. And when I am feeling down and out, your comfort gives me hope. You place kisses on my brow then softly kiss my lips. You take my hand and gently hold me tight and instantly I feel safe. When I am without faith you make me feel secure. You give me strength just by being here. I am so blessed to have you near...

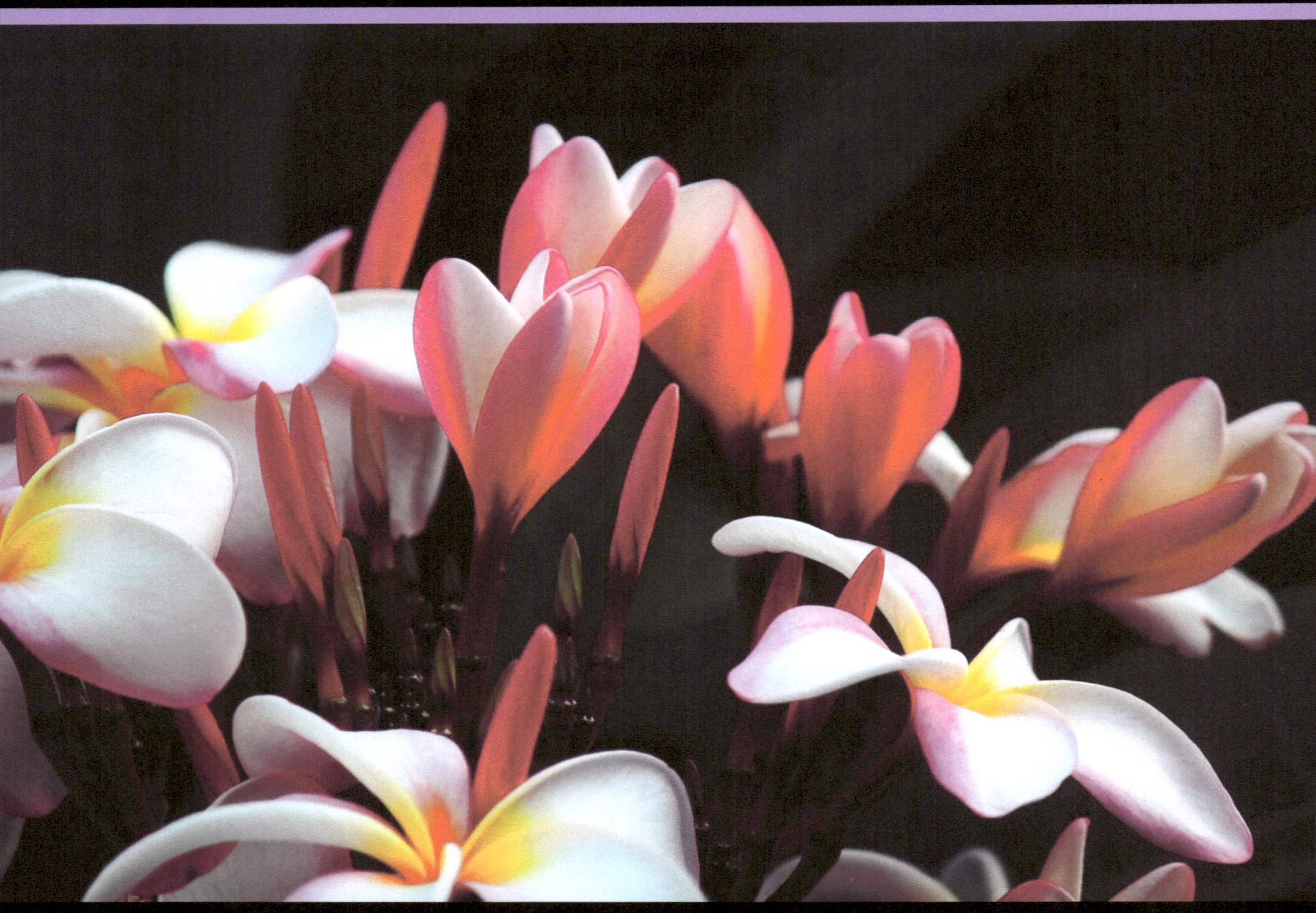

It's too late to wake you, and yet you are still on my mind. Whether you are sleeping next to me or far away on the edge of the world, you are my first thought in the morning and my last when I close my eyes. How is it that I miss you even if you are lying by my side... I guess, I will just lie here and listen to you breathe. Sweet dreams, my love. I am enamored by you even though you sleep.

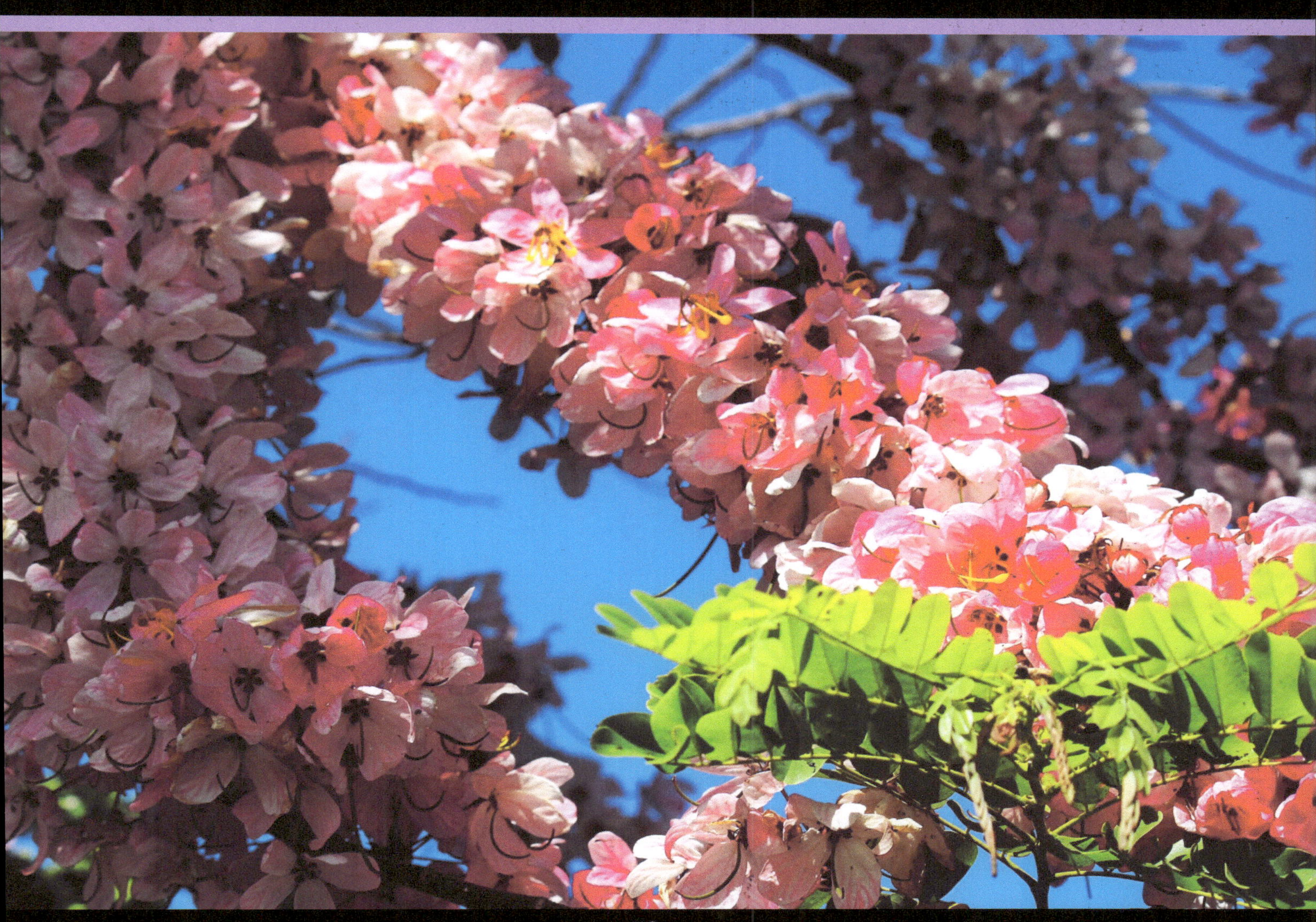

You... You tantalize my senses with your uncanny way of turning my downs into ups and my errors into gains. I appreciate who you are. You are a loving being who offers me their world. Your influence on my life is astounding and I am so thrilled just to know you. You and everything about you; from your nuanced imperfections to our heavenly carnal bliss. My heart is jumps for joy with every kiss from your lips...

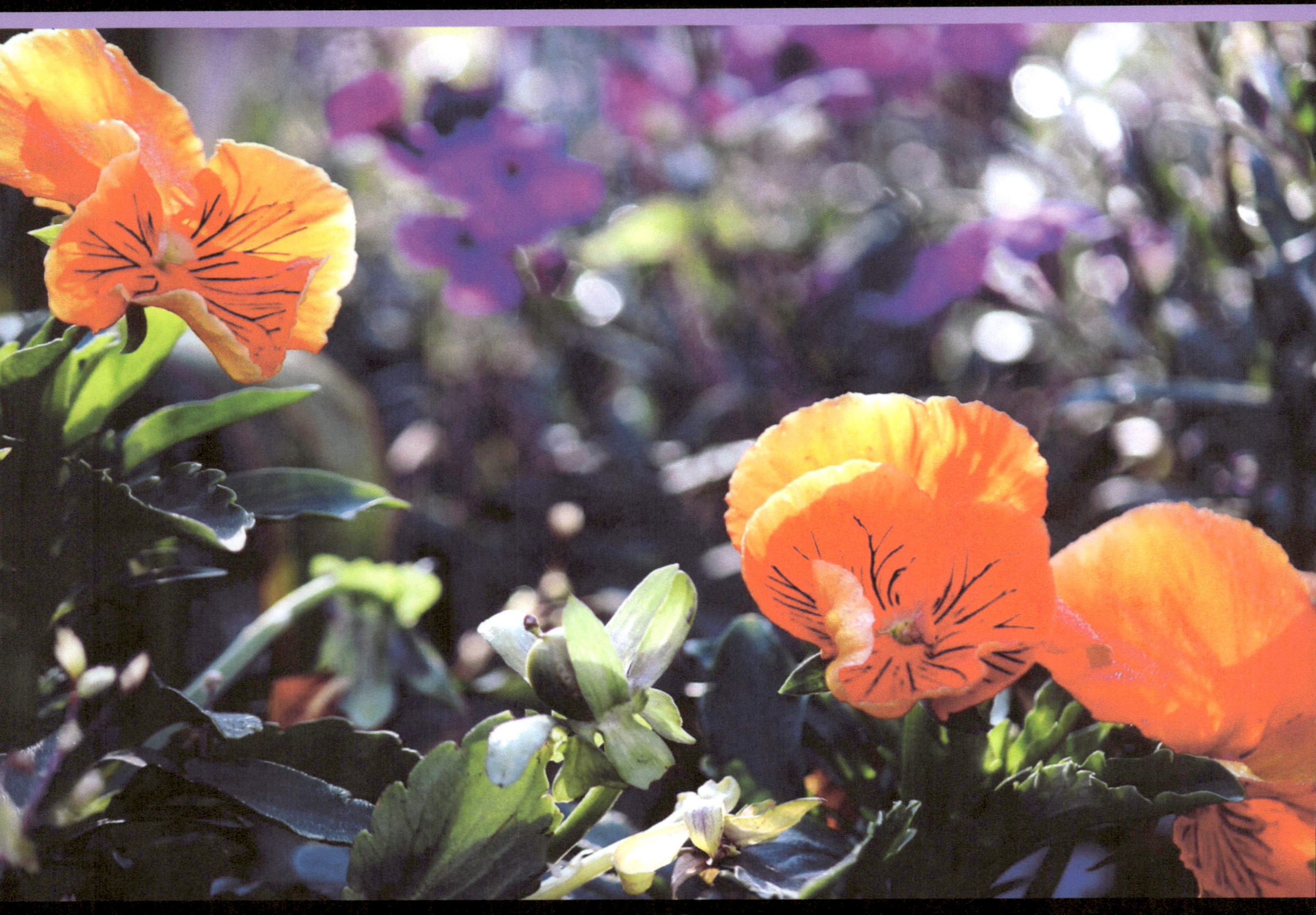

What makes anyone fall in love? Is it the warmth of your smile, the glint in your eyes? Is it the sincerity in your voice, or butterflies from your touch? Is it your words spoken in jest or a feeling of calm when you drew near? Is it the beauty found within you or how pretty you are all dressed up? Whatever it is, it moves me beyond my wildest dreams. There is no way to describe it, except to say that I'm in love with you...

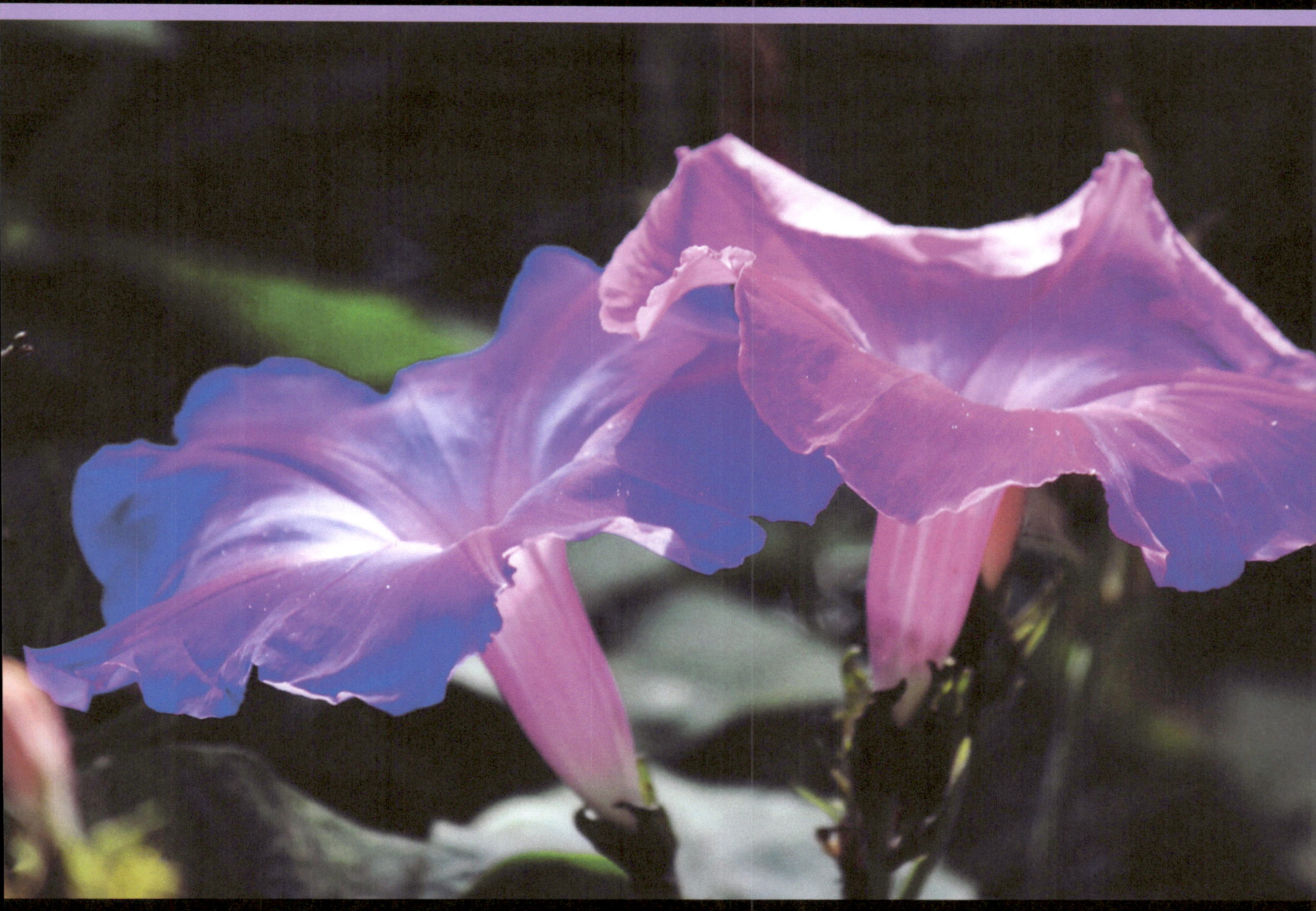

Kiss me lightly on my cheek. Tell me how much you care. I think I want to marry you, to promise you all I am. Please don't turn away from me; can't you see the love in my eyes. You doubt, but I mean every word. I want you to be mine. If you love me like you say you do, then let us prove our love is true. Marry me and be my wife. Marry me now and be the love of my life. Marry me...

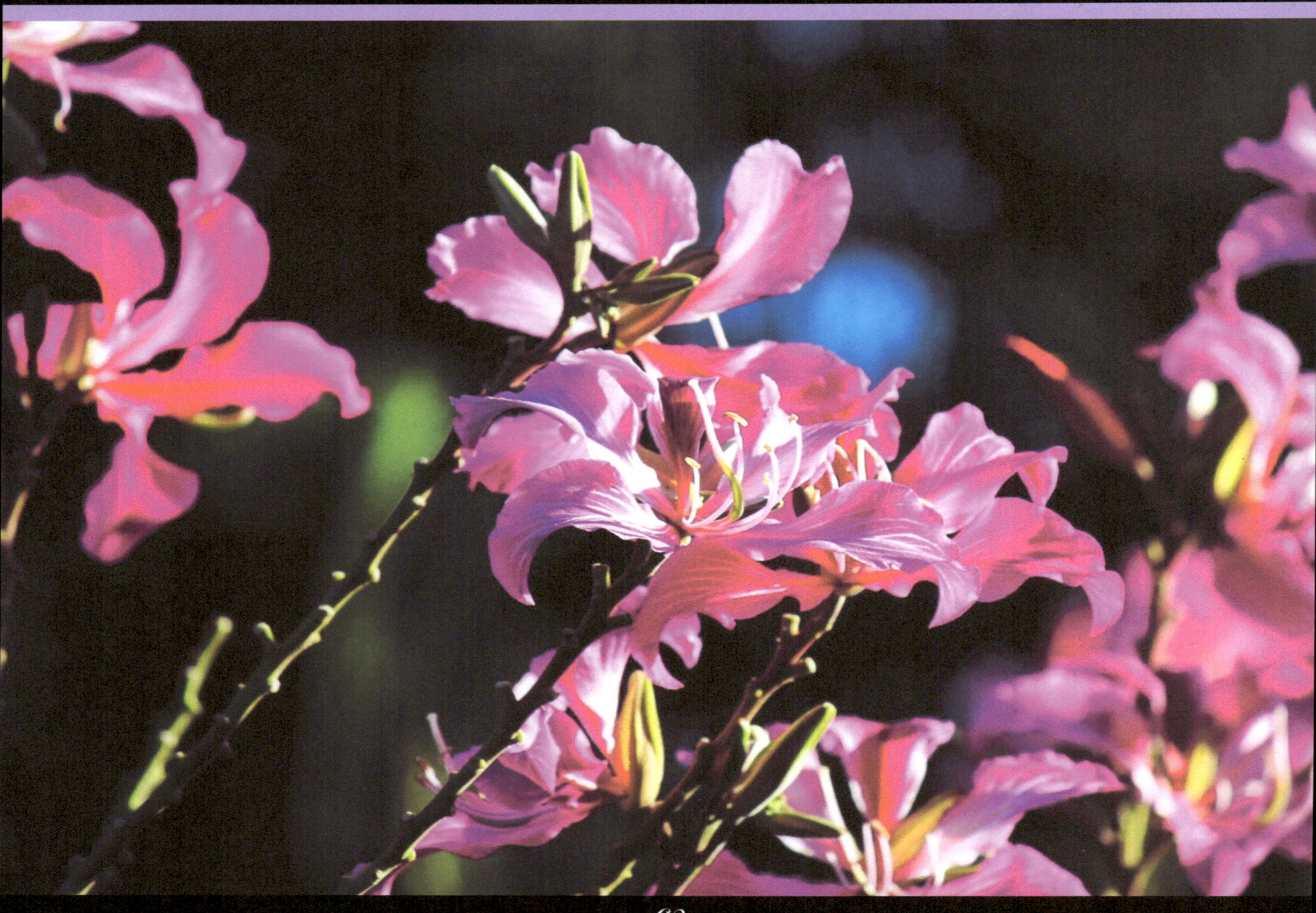

I feel your heat rising on my roving fingertips. When I touch our skin I am like a tiger ready to pounce on your sexy lips. Smoldering, swiveling are your rounded hips. Rising, falling breasts... I want to take a sip. Hmm... You taste like sweet chocolate, mocha, and crème. You've dipped yourself in honey and I am a honey bee. I'm tasting and savoring your delicious scent. I am delving in your nectar, and I am filled by your essence...

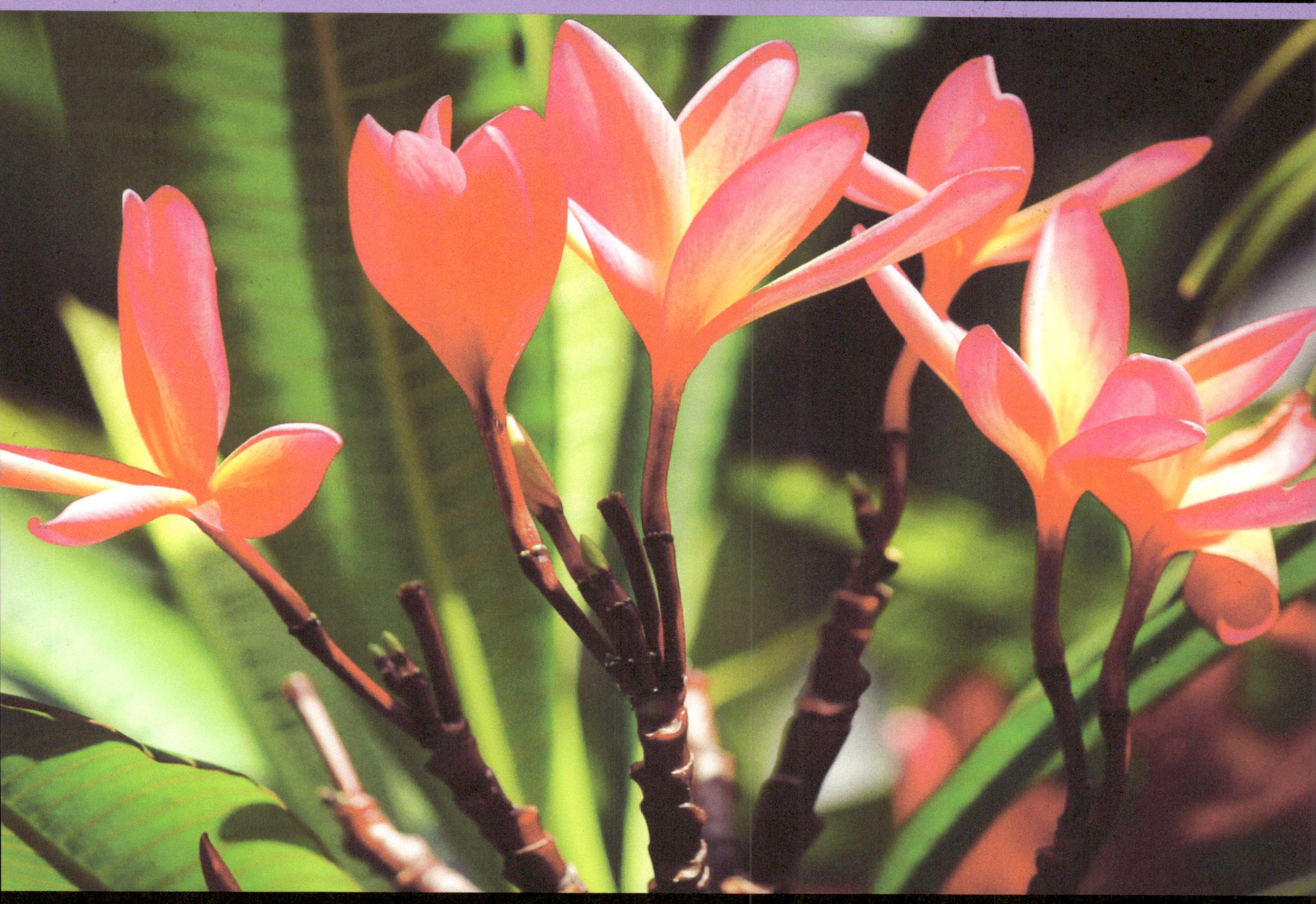

My Dearest Desire, you are playing with fire and I am ready to burn. You've lit the lamps and the candles are romancing. Black lace and nothing? Lord, have mercy, what are you wearing? Your heady scent is driving me crazy. Your tempest is high...it's overwhelming. Consume me with games of passion...Thrill me in white hot satin. Take me to your heaven with your sweet hypnotic kiss...

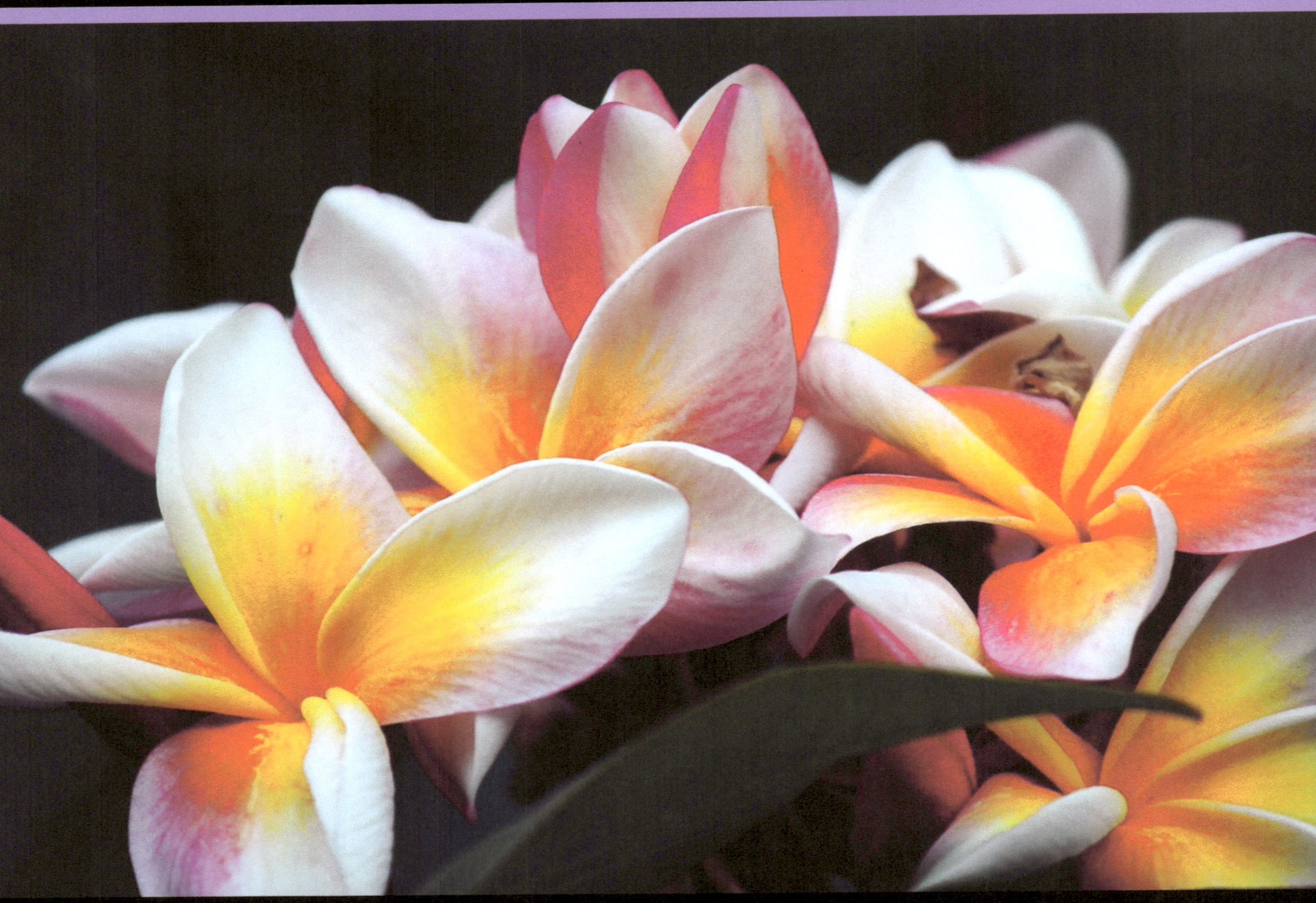

Love is a rare and beautiful flower, a soft and gentle breeze. Love is a whisper of honesty, a gentle shoulder on which one can lean. Love is an ear that listens even when nothing is said. Love never wastes your time, it gives life meaning instead... I never knew about true love until I met you. You have opened my eyes and the whole world can see. How I relish this beautiful moment, captivated by your smile, and the love you have given me...

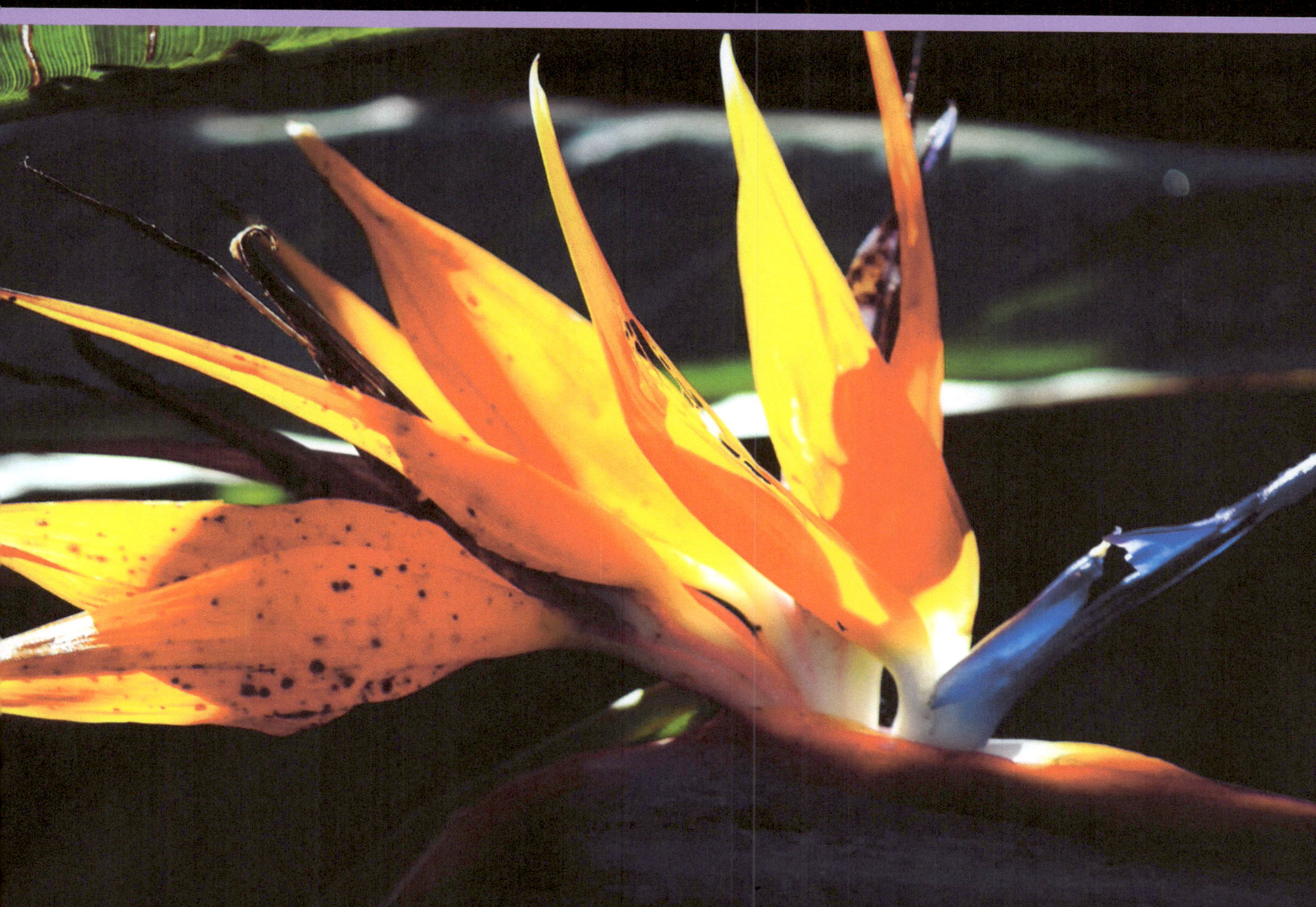

You inspire me. Just your presence in my life makes me dream. You are my light, my sunshine, my bright perfect morning, and I wake up refreshed and singing. You are my song, my perfect melody; the music in my soul that I hums repeatedly. And the joy you bring fills me, and my heart is full of laughter because I have you... You... You... So happy that I have you...

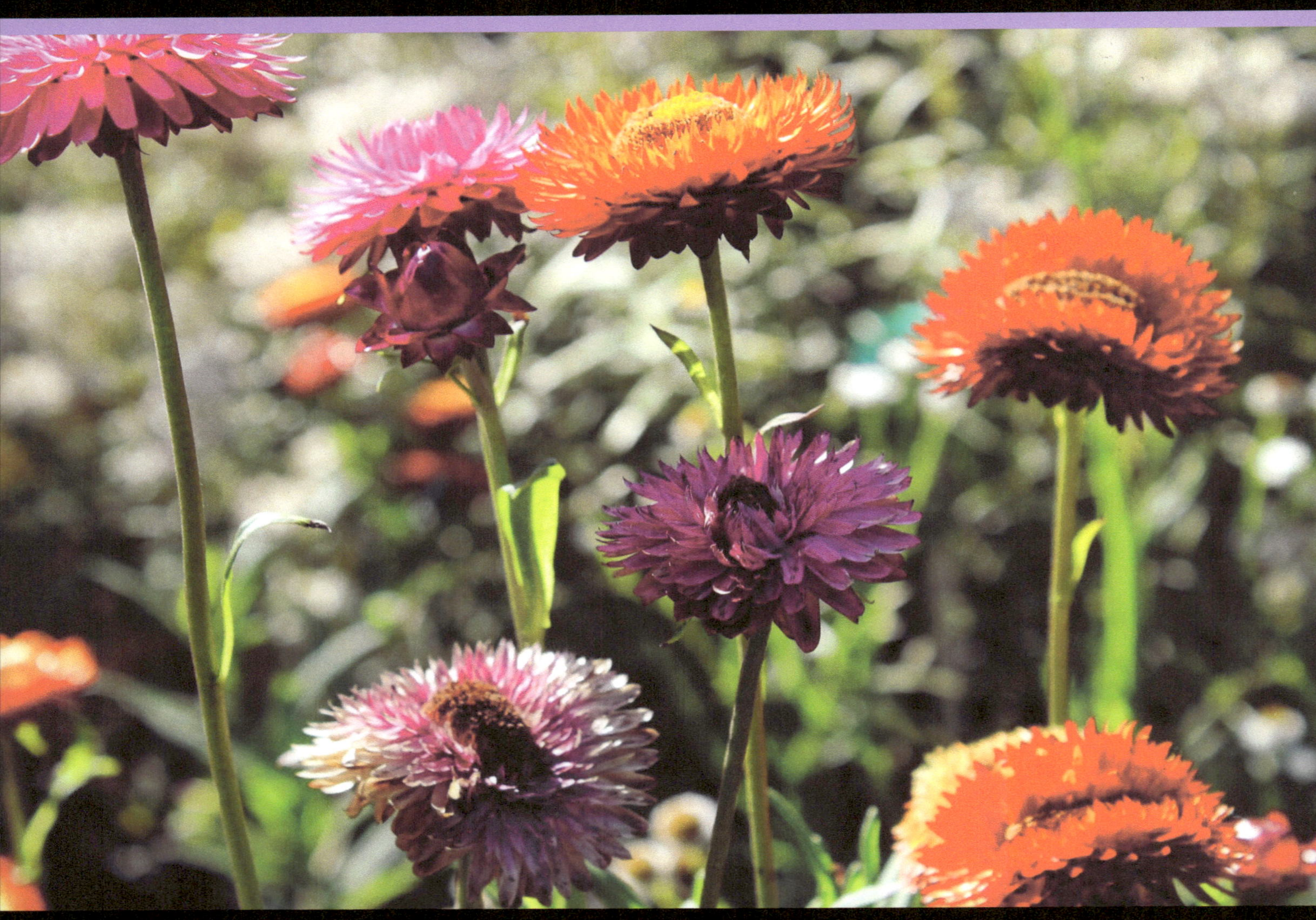

Say the word and I promise to love you forever. Through all time your kisses will be my treasure, And the riches that life will offer, no man can ever take away. This love is ours for the taking and destiny is ours in the making. And you and I shall live breathlessly without regretting... I promise you my life.

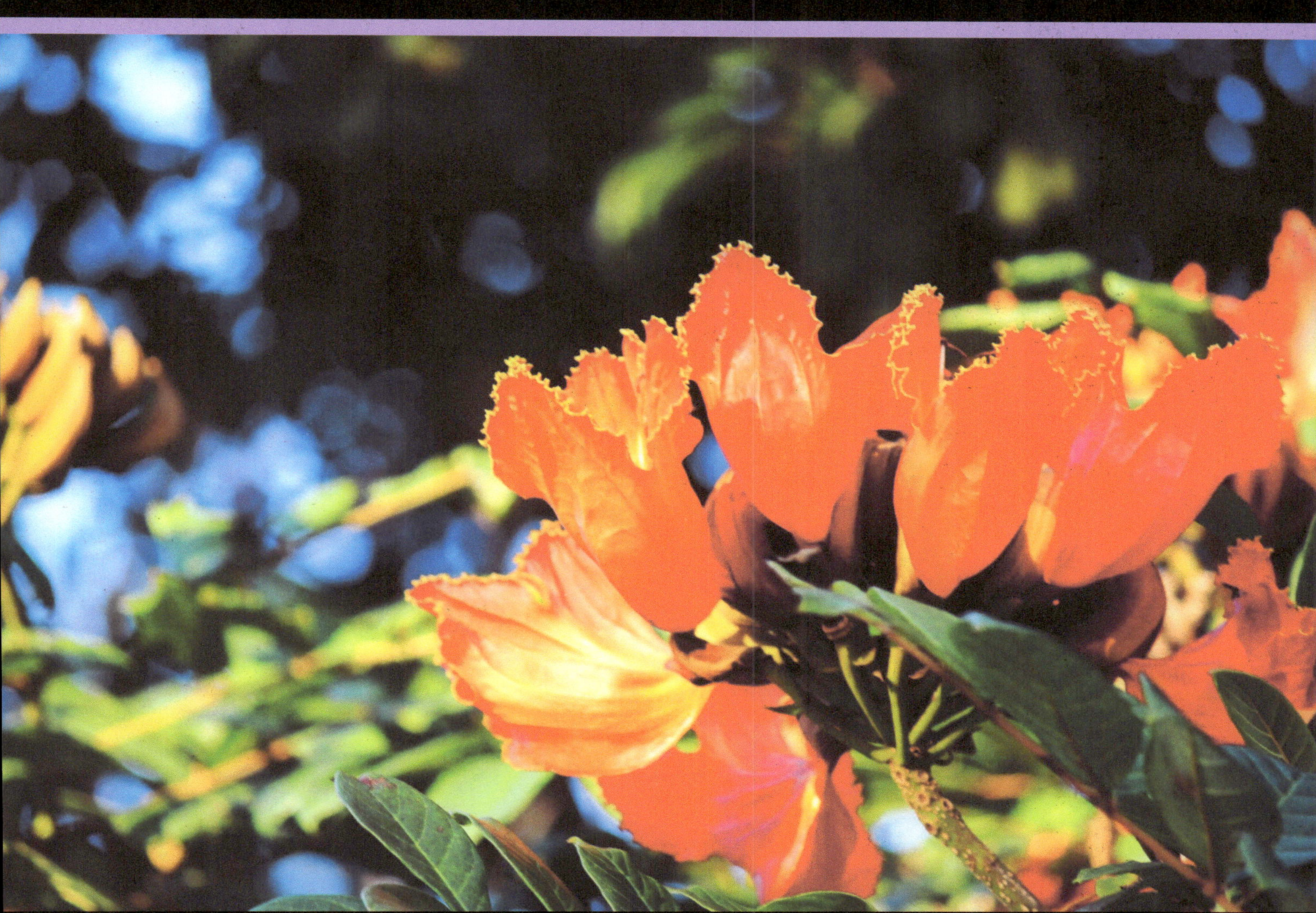

You are my gift, my heavenly prize. For surely it was love who heard my cry. Some say that it's chance that brought you my way, but there must be angels listening, because I prayed to find you. I prayed for blissful happiness and my miracle came true... There must be a God in heaven, for only perfect love could have made you...

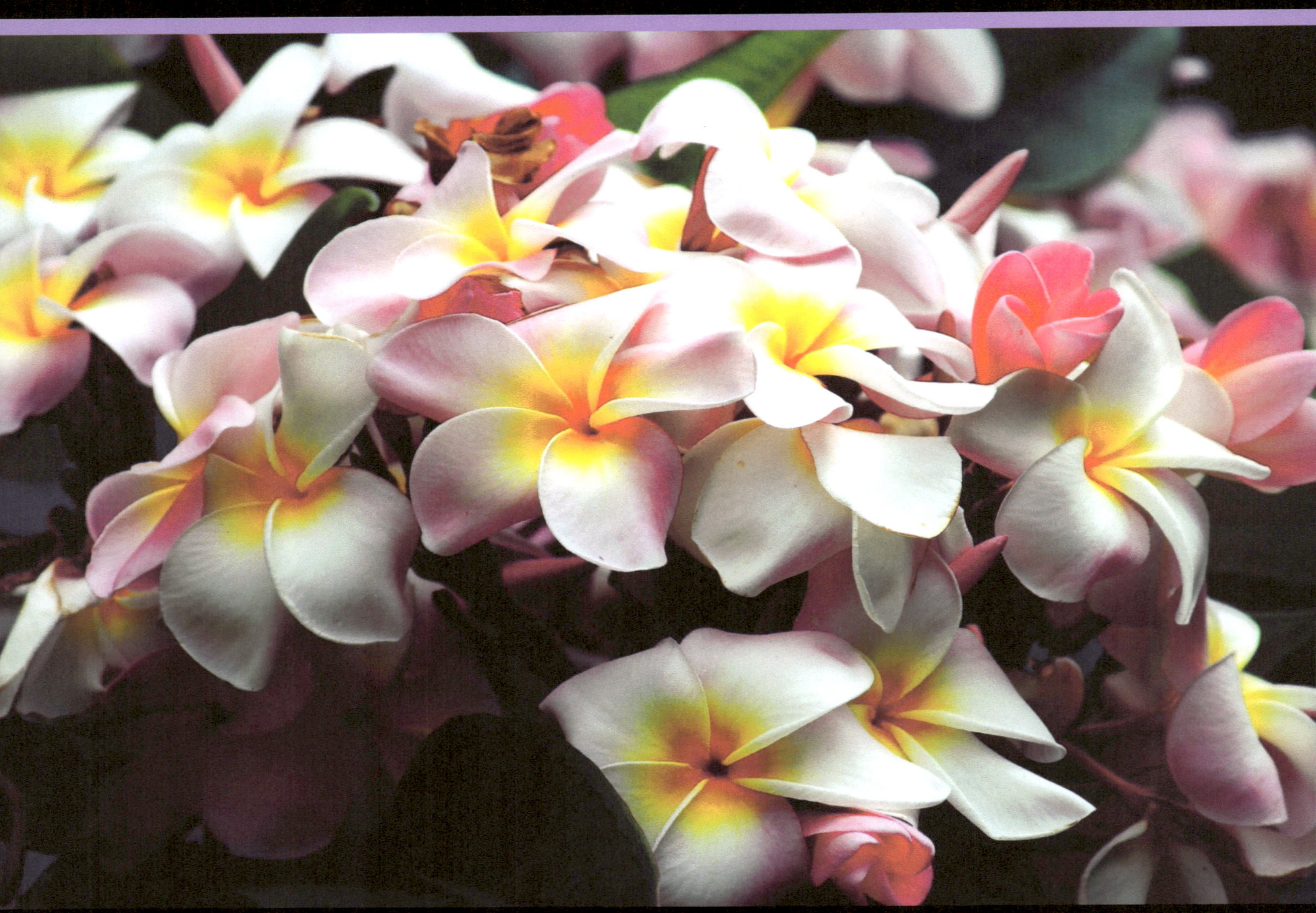

Touch my hand, my love, my divine. I am waiting for your kiss to merge with mine. Come closer, my darling, my beloved, my sweet... Feel my pulse; feel my heat. I never knew that I could want you this much. My loneliness is gone and true love is upon us... Follow me, my heart, my gentle dove into the sultry night. Here in the dark I will show you love, and I will love you immeasurably for life...

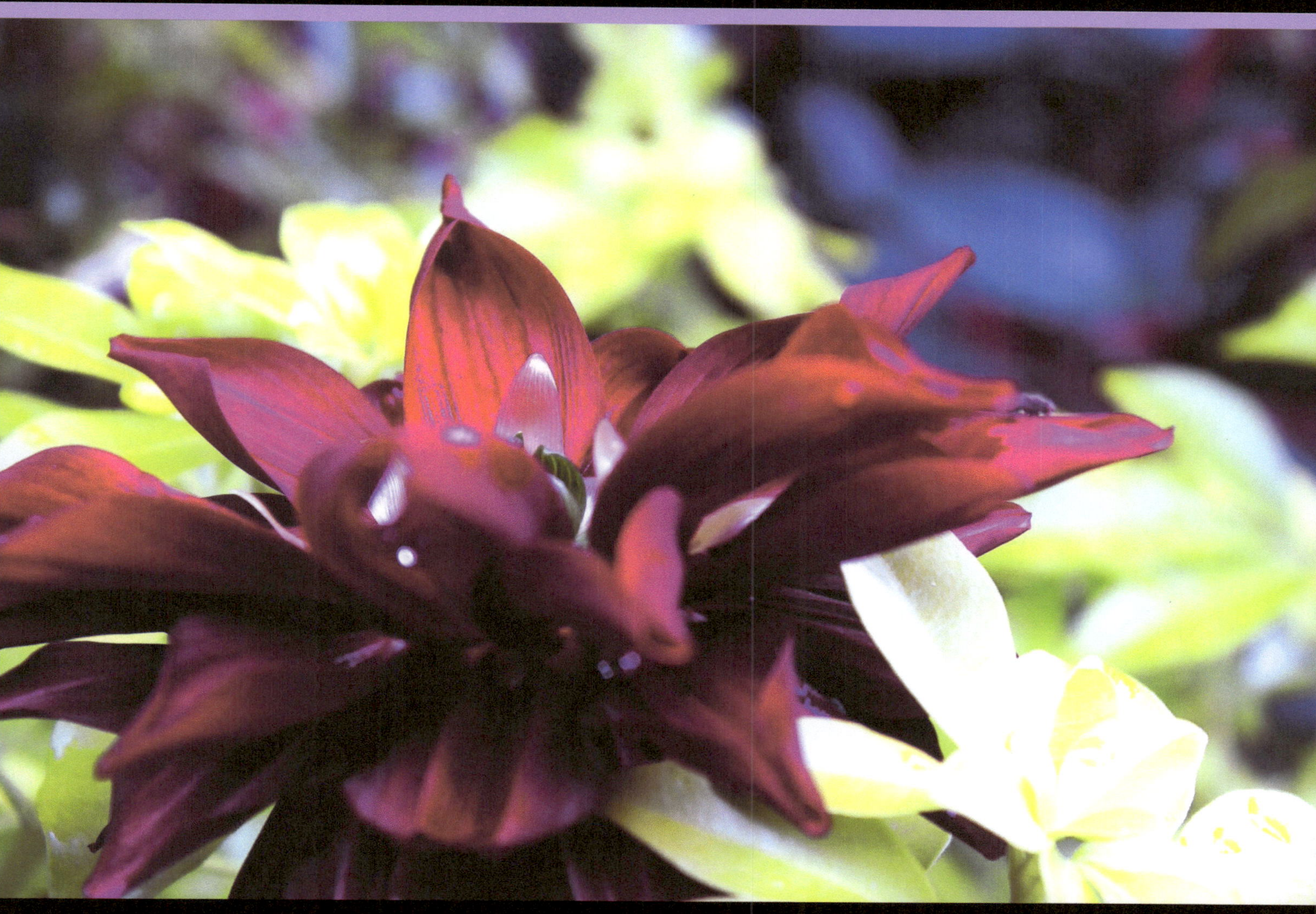

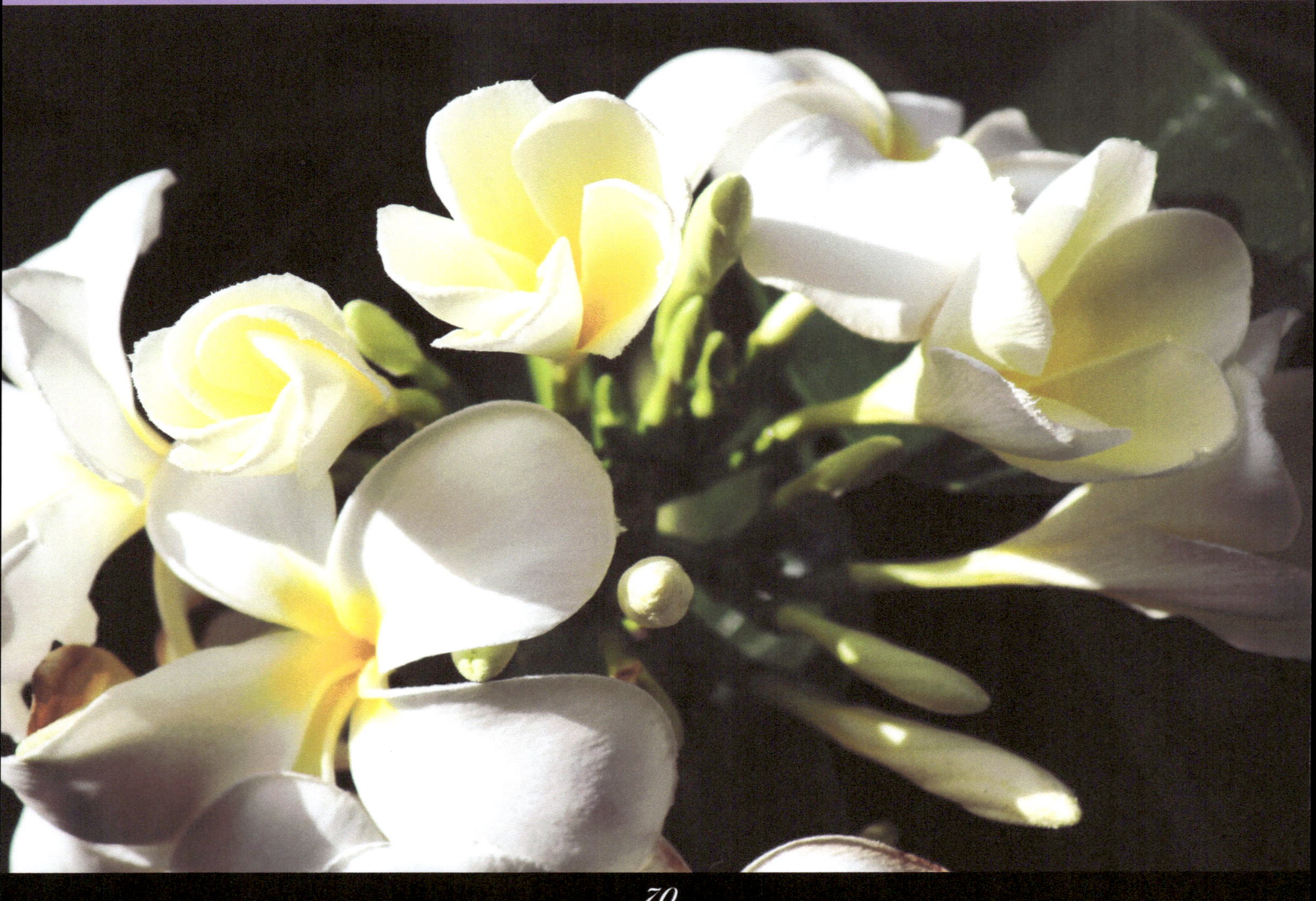

If I can inspire a heart to beat again or breathe life into a dream; hearten those who cry in the night and bring them the morning sun—then my journey was worth the tears, and I triumphed in the midst of them all...

D. Ashanti-Dubois

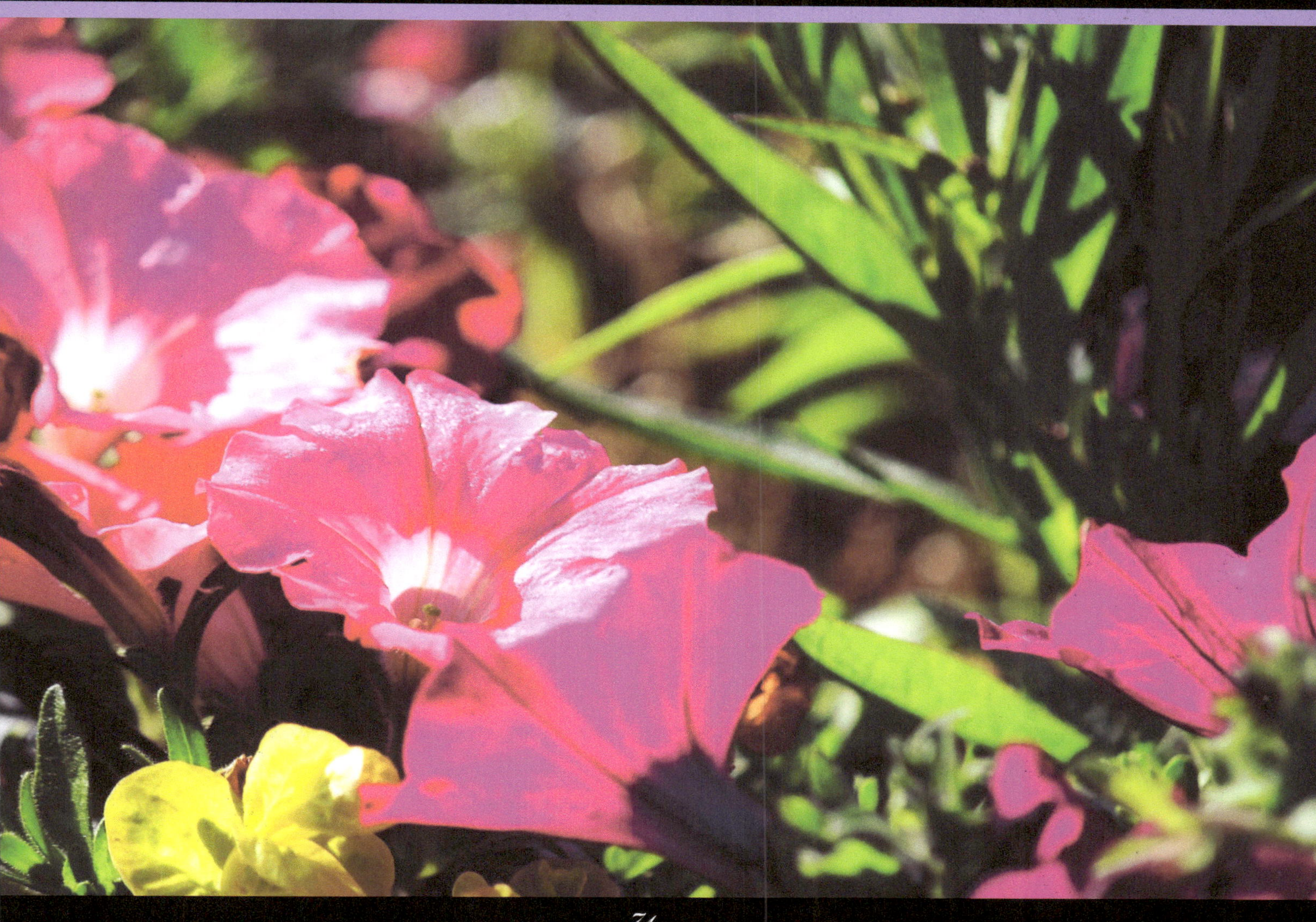

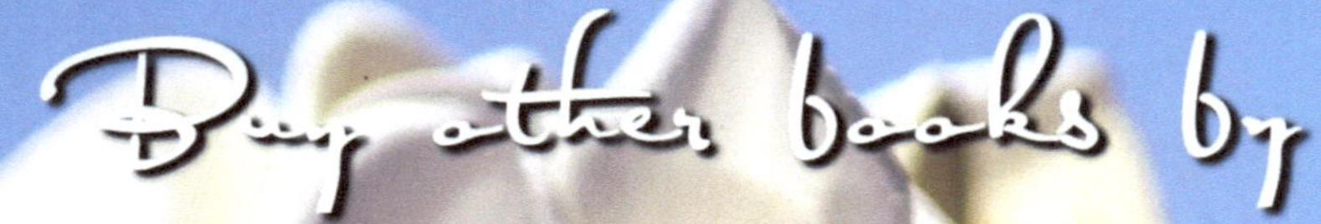

D. ASHANTI-DUBOIS

MESSAGES OF HOPE (SERIES)

WHEN YOU NEED A MIRACLE–PRAY

HEAVEN & EARTH

THE DREAM WEAVERS

My Dove Song
MYDOVESONG
PUBLISHING

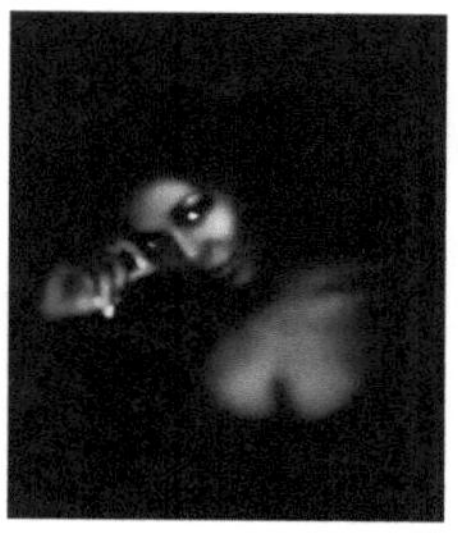

ABOUT THE AUTHOR

Author and creative artist D. Ashanti-Dubois brings light and love to the universe of literature through her latest edition, Messages d'Amour – Reflections of Love. As a multifaceted writer, photographer, vocalist, composer, graphiste, and artiste, D. Ashanti-Dubois brings a unique perspective to the world of spiritual enlightenment. After nearly two decades of living internationally and in Hawaii, her many travels have emboldened her belief in the spirit of hope, love, and humanity.

Born and raised in St. Louis, Missouri where she began her creative journey writing poetry, prose, and songs at the tender age of five, D. Ashanti-Dubois continues her artistic odyssey producing various genres of books, music, photography, and art. Her spiritual anthology, *Messages of Hope,* is a collection of beautifully written spiritual insights that will inspire and empower your life. The entire Messages of Hope series can be purchased online through Amazon.com and other vendors.

Also available: *Messages of Hope – Words to Uplift the Human Spirit:* An uplifting book of 33 inspire messages and 36 exercises to heal your life with more than 150 gorgeous original photographs. *Heaven & Earth – Paradise Et La Terre:* A collection of spiritual poetic odes with gorgeous scenic photography. *When You Need A Miracle – Pray:* A magnificent collection of meditations and prayers to uplift the weary heart with beautiful more photographs.

For more books available by D. Ashanti-Dubois visit www.mydovesong.com. Look for other editions scheduled to be released in the coming years.

www.ingramcontent.com/pod-product-compliance
Lightning Source LLC
LaVergne TN
LVHW070142110826
845147LV00002B/312

9780692022023